REVOLUTIONARY
HILLBILLY

REVOLUTIONARY
HILLBILLY

Notes From The Struggle
On The Edge Of The Rainbow

by
Hy Thurman
CO-FOUNDER OF THE YOUNG PATRIOTS ORGANIZATION

INTRODUCTION BY
Amy Sonnie and James Tracy

REGENT PRESS
Berkeley, California
2020

Copyright © 2020 by Dr. Hy Thurman

[Paperback]
ISBN 13: 978-1-58790-551-3
ISBN 10: 1-58790-551-5

[E-Book]
ISBN 13: 978-1-58790-552-0
ISBN 10: 1-58790-552-3

Library of Congress Control Cataloging-in-Publication Data
Names: Thurman, Hy, 1950- author.
Title: Revolutionary hillbilly : notes from the struggle on the edge of the
  rainbow / by Hy Thurman ; introduction by Amy Sonnie & James Tracy.
Description: First edition. | Berkeley, California : Regent Press, 2020. |
  Summary: "
Identifiers: LCCN 2020050015 (print) | LCCN 2020050016 (ebook) | ISBN
  9781587905513 (trade paperback) | ISBN 9781587905520 (ebook)
Subjects: LCSH: Thurman, Hy, 1950- | Young Patriots Organization. | Civic
  leaders--United States--Biography. | Political activists--United
  States--Biography. | Community organization--United
  States--History--20th century. | Civil rights--United
  States--History--20th century. | Social movements--United
  States--History--20th century. | Social justice--United
  States--History--20th century.
Classification: LCC HN90.C6 T488 2020 (print) | LCC HN90.C6 (ebook) | DDC
  323.092--dc23
LC record available at https://lccn.loc.gov/2020050015
LC ebook record available at https://lccn.loc.gov/2020050016

Photographs pages 94-103 by Bob Rehak originally published in:
UPTOWN: Portrait of a Chicago Neighborhood in the Mid-1970s
Copyright © 2013 Rehak Creative Services, Inc.

Iconic image of Hy Thurman by Miriam Klein Stahl:
https://www.miriamkleinstahl.com

Cover Design: James Tracy

First Edition

1 2 3 4 5 6 7 8 9 10

Manufactured in the U.S.A.
REGENT PRESS
Berkeley, California
www.regentpress.net

Table of Contents

Foreword

by Amy Sonnie and James Tracy

The book you have in your hands is a history book, an organizer's notebook, and an autobiography. These are stories of unity against poverty and racism. Hy Thurman is a hillbilly and a revolutionary organizer. As a co-founder of the Young Patriots Organization, Thurman helped organize poor white communities in alliance with the Illinois Black Panther Party and Young Lords Organization during the Sixties. He is an educator who got his schooling in the fields of Tennessee, his PhD on the streets of Chicago, and his hunger for justice in the back of a patrol car.

We have been waiting decades for this book. As young activists, the Patriots' legacy — documented only in footnotes and a few artifacts — sparked our ten-year journey to answer the question: How does a group of poor white hillbillies come to stand arm in arm with Black Panthers and Young Lords under the banner of a Rainbow Coalition? The answers took us beyond Chicago and back again as we wrote *Hillbilly Nationalists, Urban Race Rebels and Black Power*. As soon as we met Hy Thurman, we knew. His book — this book — was necessary.

~ ~ ~

The allies within the Original Rainbow Coalition had much in common: the fight against urban renewal and slum conditions, lack of healthcare, employment discrimination, and experiences of brutal police violence. The fact that they were able to work together over many years is a testament to both the tenor of the revolutionary times and the lifelong political commitment they forged, independently and together.

The Patriots were honest in confronting the deep racism in their community and equally frustrated that some middle-class organizers often considered poor whites a "lost cause." The Patriots and their close collaborators understood that placing disproportionate blame on poor white people ignores the reality of racialized capitalism and thwarts the opportunity to organize.

This is why the Patriots are worth studying. They attempted to build a political practice rooted in class solidarity with Black Power and Third World Liberation while directly addressing legacies of racism and colonialism. They were part of an informal tendency with groups like Rising Up Angry, White Lightning, the Intercommunal Survival Committee, and October 4th Organization, the Young Patriots took responsibility to organize their own community in the North's most segregated city, while working toward collective liberation.

~ ~ ~

Hy Thurman remains on the frontlines today. We see Thurman in Ray Santisteban's documentary, *The First Rainbow Coalition*, participating in a counter-mobilization against Neo-Nazis in 2017. He has organized a new chapter of the Young Patriots in Alabama and is a sought-after speaker across the United States. In 2020, he launched the Northern Alabama School For Organizers reflecting his commitment to accessible political education for all. Like many surviving members of the Rainbow Coalition, he never abandoned his values, even during the years state repression forced many radicals into hiding.

Hy is a revolutionary hillbilly. When Hollywood churns out propaganda naming hillbillies as ignorant and lazy, turn to this book. When you hear progressive activists deriding "rednecks" with a fake southern accent, return to this book. Tell them about the Young Patriots. Introduce them to Hy Thurman. Show them the stories of another reality — the radical songs of the South written in tent cities, picket lines, and pool halls.

These are the stories we went looking for to guide our own activism. The leaders we met — named throughout this book — continue to teach us. Draw what lessons you may. Perhaps the most important one is the evidence of possibilities beyond simple Red and Blue states, Black and White divisions. When populist moments arise, it is always the groundwork laid by organizers determining the story's arc. Let Hy Thurman's story show us the way from the front-porch of hatred toward the bright morning of new solidarities.

— Amy Sonnie and James Tracy
Oakland, California
November 2020

Introduction: The Making of A Revolutionary Hillbilly

"When we say South, we mean south of the Canadian border."
— MALCOLM X, 1964

"The United States has always maintained a white under-class whose role in the greater scheme of things has been to cushion national economic shocks through the disposability of their labor, with occasional time off to serve as bullet magnets in the defense of their empire. — JOE BAGEANT
RAINBOW PIE: A MEMOIR OF REDNECK AMERICA

All of my life I have been a Hillbilly. Since 1967, I have been a Revolutionary Hillbilly. Over the past five decades of my life, I have waged a war against poverty and racial injustices. I was a founding member of the Young Patriots Organization (YPO). We were a group of Southern white youth dedicated to serving and defending our community — an impoverished neighborhood called Uptown in Chicago. We were Southerners whose families migrated to Chicago's Uptown neighborhood looking for work. We came to form part of the First Rainbow Coalition, working together with the Black Panthers and the Puerto Rican Young Lords. The Rainbow Coalition built unity across the color lines starting with our common experiences with poverty.

The Patriots fought for freedom and equality in a city that denied us both. We fought against racism, police brutality, and city planners who administered the urban renewal program to force poor people out of their homes. Modeled after the Black Panther Party for Self-Defense, we organized free health services, breakfast for children programs, food pantries and legal services for the poor in Uptown.

Until recently, the Patriots' history was only cited in the footnotes of books about the Students for a Democratic Society (SDS), the Black Panther Party, and the New Left. In recent years, there have been two books which have uncovered parts of this history. *Hillbilly Nationalists, Urban Race Rebels and Black Power: Community Organizing in Radical Times* by Amy Sonnie and James Tracy were the first writers to take our legacy seriously. *From the Bullet to the Ballot: The Illinois Chapter of the Black Panther Party and Racial Coalition Politics in Chicago* by Jakobi Williams examined the original Rainbow Coalition's political platform and the leadership of Black Panther Deputy Chairman Fred Hampton.

Throughout the years as a radical organizer, I have taken notes about what I have seen. I want to explain who we were as revolutionary people, why we started the Patriots, and what we hoped to accomplish. My work stems from my experiences as a poor person from the South. It draws on my life in Uptown and the challenges I personally faced as a result of police brutality, poverty, class hatred and other forms of harassment, and how it refined my ability to organize.

Most importantly, I attempt to preserve the history of a forgotten people dealing with the brutal conditions of migration, starvation, slum living, death, disease, classism, racism, police brutality and even murder. We were a struggling people fighting to keep our identity and dignity in a city that would not allow us to assimilate, and would not accept us when we tried. I want to demonstrate how a group of poor people, uneducated to the process and techniques of organizing, stepped up to demand to be heard and refused to be victims of an oppressive system.

This book is my attempt to take these notes from my notebook so that they can be of use to the next generation of activists. This generation, like mine before, has to confront the massive inequality and the resurgence of organized white supremacy. They also have in front of them the task of facing down an environmental catastrophe. I hope that by sharing my experiences — the successes and failures of organizing — that this book might make their work a little easier.

— *Hy Thurman,*
Huntsville, Alabama 2020

Life in Appalachia

The first major influences on me becoming a lifelong activist was being raised in the poverty-stricken South. In the remote, underdeveloped regions of Appalachia in the 1950's and 1960's, poverty was so widespread that people were experiencing hunger on a daily basis, and the results of malnutrition were catastrophic. Since these regions collected very little taxes, they were denied government funds to change living conditions. Government programs in education and job training were unattainable to those in the mountainous regions due to unmaintained roads that prevented industry to expand into the small towns, while it was difficult for many to travel to other towns to seek jobs — many did not own automobiles.

Some refer to their past as the "good old days" — there was no such thing for me and my community. With declining health, and a lack of education and employable skills to escape poverty, my mother tried her best to provide for her children. During the harvest season, we would rise early before daybreak to work in the fields (growing beans, strawberries, corn, tomatoes and gathering hay) to survive. My twin brother and I were three years old when we started working in the fields alongside our four sibling and mother.

My older sisters would babysit us until we got old enough to take care of ourselves. They would take turns so there would be no interruptions in the field work. I am to this day haunted by my mother`s tears and apologies that she had no means of providing a better life for us. It was a miserable existence with the body pains that came with the blistering heat and strenuous field work. There were other families working alongside us who were as poverty-stricken as we were.

The wife or children of the owner of the field would arrive daily with a tub of ice filled with soft drinks, water and home cooked snacks. None of which were free to workers.

The purchase of drinks and snacks would take up most of our daily wages, which wasn't enough to survive on. Water was available as a courtesy. As I got older, I would often look on the hill from the field and see the field owner's house with its beautiful green yard, swing sets and outside tables, where he and his family would sit in the evenings and enjoy the fruits of their labor ... and mine as well. "What would it be like to live like that?" I would wonder.

At the end of the day, we would pool our daily wages to come up with an amount that would assure us eating that evening, and helped supplement rent on our run-down shack. Because of the inadequate maintenance on the shacks, we would at times put cardboard and newspaper on the inside walls to keep the cold air out. When we were short on rent, we would sometimes move to another shack. I remember we would have to cook outside on a makeshift grill when our wood stove would wear out. Electricity was luxury we couldn't afford.

We considered ourselves lucky when blackberries and raspberries were in season because we could harvest them and sell them for one hundred percent profit or preserve them. When we had time, we would plant vegetables and raise a few chickens. Until I got older, my brothers would sometime hunt squirrel and rabbit for our supper. Fish was a constant staple in our home.

My older sister and my mother both wore the same shoe size, and for many years shared shoes. When my mother had to take a trip to town, she would wear the shoes. During the summer months, when my twin and I were very young, we did not wear shoes. Other siblings

wore cheap shoes to work in the fields. My older sister
remembers that when she was a child — due to a lack of
beds — she would sleep in a dresser drawer until she got
older and outgrew it. Most clothes were hand-me-downs.
As my twin and I were the youngest, we had very little
wearable clothes because they were so worn out by the
time they reached us.

Small Town Justice

Growing up in a small town made many poor whites and blacks a target for crimes by the local cops. They would arrest and falsely accuse young men and women for crimes that were committed by the more privileged in the county. My family was no exception to false accusations. Several times the cops picked me and my brothers up for questioning about a crime, even though we were nowhere near where they were committed. Due to this treatment, we were treated with indifference and harassed by other members of the county.

In 1965, I was accused of stealing money from vending machines in the town. I had proof that on the date of the crime I was not near the crime scene. Still, I was accused of being the lookout for crimes on other crimes, in case the cops would appear. Although the cops could not charge me, they did arrest my twin brother and sentenced him to one-year confinement in a juvenile detention facility in Nashville.

In 1966, the owner of a roadside truck stop reported the theft of an expensive horse saddle from his place of business. A friend and I were detained by the County Sheriff, who accused us of stealing the saddle. The sheriff demanded to examine one of my shoes. I found it comical when he stated that the dry mud on my shoe matched the mud behind the truck stop. In fact, the same soil was found all over the state of Tennessee. He informed us that he had witnesses who saw us steal the saddle.

The saddle was allegedly taken from the kitchen of the truck stop that was open 24-hours a day, all year round. Apparently, it was closed for one night when the saddle was taken. According to Sheriff Thurman, my friend and I were observed entering through a restroom window in the rear of the building around 2 a.m. that morning, and were later seen removing the saddle from the building through the same window. My friend informed the sheriff that we had been in the bathroom before and that the window was too small to put the saddle through. He ignored us when we informed him that we had an alibi for the period of time the crime was committed. And he ignored us when we asked for the names of the witnesses and what they were doing in a wooded area behind the truck stop at that time of the morning.

We were given twenty-four hours to return the saddle or we would be charged with the crime. When my friend and I tried to talk to the owner of the saddle, we were met by one of his hired men, someone known to be connected with the Southern Mafia, who pointed a revolver at us and said, "If you don't return the saddle, I will hunt you down and take care of the situation." We decided to lay low for a few days knowing that the sheriff would be searching for us. Several days later, we heard that someone from another town in the county had been charged with the crime.

The most disturbing accusation came in late 1966 when I was picked up and questioned for being a part of the rape of a teenage girl by three assailants. She identified the attackers as being in their late teens to early twenties. She stated that one was wearing a brown jacket. I was wearing a brown jacket when I was picked up. The cops informed the girl's parents that they had picked up a suspect, and asked them to come to the station to identify him. Fortunately, our families were friends and I was cleared as a suspect. When I left the station, a cop said, "You got away this time but we will get you the next time." No one was ever charged with the crime. The girl and her family eventually moved back to Michigan.

Even my older sister could not escape police harassment. When she was fifteen, she had an uncomfortable experience with a cop when he inappropriately touched her as he was searching her. She fought back by attacking him, and scratched both sides of his face. She believed that by that by fighting back, she could avoid being charged for assaulting a police officer, because he would have to explain his behavior.

Due to the constant police harassment and my family's reputation, I knew that it was just a matter of time before I would be serving jail time. I started making plans to join the military on my seventeenth birthday in February of 1967. Fortunately, for me, my older brother, who lived in Chicago, visited later that month and. Within a matter of days, I was in Chicago.

The Great Migration

arrived to Chicago in March of 1967 at the age of seventeen to join my brother Ralph, who migrated five years earlier to escape the harshness of poverty, classism, lack of jobs and the collapse of the farming economy due to mechanization of farms in the South. I was also hoping to escape police harassment and class hatred in my home town. I had heard that Chicago was the "promised land," that life was better up north, and that jobs were abundant for those who were willing to work.

Ralph encouraged me to stay in Tennessee because living in Chicago was not what I had heard it to be. "There is no promised land. Hillbillies are not liked nor welcomed in Chicago," he warned. He urged me to prepare myself for the difficult circumstances I would surely encounter in the city. But he agreed that if I had made up my mind about leaving our home town, then I could go to Chicago and stay with him. I'm glad that I went to Chicago, but my brother was absolutely correct. All of the problems he warned me about confronted me shortly after I arrived in Chicago.

I was in total cultural shock when I arrived in Uptown. The southern dialect, country music and the Confederate flag were the only identifiable remnants of the southern culture I left behind. There was a shortage of housing, and yet many apartment buildings were falling apart and were boarded up. Trees and grass were practically non-existent. Children played in the street alongside passed out drunks. The air smelled of urine and garbage. Glass and debris littered streets crowded with people. The congestion increased later, when hundreds of patients were released from mental health institutions and placed in Uptown, where many begged for money, drugs, alcohol and food. Shop owners and street people would stare at me as I passed and would not respond when I greeted them, as was our Southern custom. There were no open spaces and abandoned vehicles lined many of the streets.

There was also a heavy police presence patrolling the street. Within my first week in Chicago, I witnessed two cops beating an elderly man, as well as a number of street fights and more incidents of police harassment.

The usual hospitality that I was accustomed to was missing. Almost everyone appeared to be stressed and unfriendly. Many young guys were wearing leather jackets and appeared to be angry and unhappy. Most children wore worn-out clothing, and some begged for money. This was not what I imagined Chicago to be. My attraction to Chicago was how it was portrayed in books and television as an exciting gangster town, full of glamor and beautiful people, with tall buildings on the lakefront.

I believed that anyone could get rich in Chicago. The Gold Coast was there for everyone, and they all could share in Chicago`s treasures. I learned quickly that the people, buildings, lakefront and promised land were there — along with the gangsters — but the riches were there only for a few, and they did not live in Uptown. I discovered later that other southern migrants had the same disappointing dream.

The majority of the southerners came from mining regions after losing their jobs due to closed or mechanized coal mines. Others came from regions where textile mills closed due to the import of foreign materials and products, against which the southern mills could not compete. Farmers were forced to leave their land because of mechanized farming, or because their farms were repossessed by banks. Major agricultural corporations that bought repossessed farms mechanized them, allowing them to undercut prices and run the small farmer out of business. Others were victims of shuttered coal mines or black lung disease from working in the mines.

Uptown is located on the north side of Chicago. According to Rodger Guy in his book *From Diversity to Unity: Southern and Appalachian Migrants in Uptown Chicago, 1950-1970,* It was home to one of the largest urban populations of southern whites in the United States (60% of the neighborhood had come from the South). Founded in 1920, Uptown was once the richest business district in Chicago. It boasts of a Frank Lloyd Wright residence, and many prominent poets and writers once called it home. The author Studs Terkel and George R.R. Martin lived in Uptown. The community treasured the Uptown Theater which seats over 4,000 beneath an ornate ceiling over eight stories tall. The Aragon Ballroom was host to the most famous entertainers in the country. Benny Goodman, Lawrence Welk and Frank Sinatra were only a few headliners. In the 1960's, it became the Cheetah Club and featured the best musicians in the world, such as The Dells and The Ohio Express.

Uptown is also known infamously for the gangster Al Capone's Green Mill Night Club that had moving walls in its basement, where he could quickly conceal a gambling casino. If the club was raided by the cops, people could escape through an underground tunnel that emerged in the nearby Aragon Ballroom, also home to the largest shopping district in Chicago. Essanay Studios made Chicago a movie hub at the time, and the best silent movies, such as Charlie Chaplin's "The Little Tramp," were filmed there. After World War II, the movie industry moved to California and found a more favorable climate.

Residential housing sub-divisions were being built in suburban areas, attracting city dwellers who wanted a safer environment and less crowded communities. This migration left many apartments vacant in Uptown. Absentee landlords became the norm, and many buildings were divided into small, low-income efficiency apartments requiring no lease or rent deposits. Many apartments could be rented by the week. Absentee landlords discovered a very profitable market by not maintaining the apartments and renting to poor migrants from the South and other parts of the world. Over a number of years, the city's crown jewel, Uptown, turned into one of the worst slums in Chicago.

Almost all arriving southerners were under-educated and possessed skills that were not needed in an urban environment. As one resident told Nancy Hollander and Todd Gitlin in *Uptown, Poor Whites In Chicago*, "You can't grow a garden in concrete." Furthermore, for those arriving in Uptown with black lung disease, brown lung disease or tuberculosis were not prepared for living in a city that was not only foreign to them culturally, but also very hostile physically, mentally and economically.

Absentee landlords were generally unwilling to pay to repair the boilers or for the coal needed to heat the buildings. Many apartments had little or no heat in the winter, and no air conditioning in the hot Chicago summers. Water pipes would sometimes freeze and burst, creating additional problems. Frostbite was not uncommon. Cold conditions caused severe, and sometimes fatal, complications for people with black or brown lung disease, tuberculosis and other respiratory illnesses, resulting in many people becoming afflicted with bronchitis and pneumonia.

Inhumane living conditions were allowed to continue in Uptown and other Chicago slum areas because the people living in these neighborhoods were involved in a class struggle with the more affluent residents of the city. Poor people were treated as if they were insignificant and had no value. The city government chose to ignore the problems of slum living, refusing to designate any funding to maintain the poor neighborhoods. Meanwhile, the people of Chicago did not get a clear picture of slum conditions, because the major news media was controlled by Mayor Richard J. Daley, who did not want the truth to be printed.

Many buildings were not fit to live in. City building and health department inspectors were eager to ignore violations and take bribes. Owners were allowed to keep receiving rent payments without doing any repairs to their properties. Since the owners refused to paint the apartments, residents were exposed to harmful lead-based paint long after it was deemed a danger to the public. I witnessed many residents heating bricks, wrapping them in cloth, and placing them at their feet to keep warm at night. Sometimes fires broke out as desperate residents tried lighting non-functional fireplaces to fight off the deadly cold.

Most buildings were cockroach and rat infested. One night, I was awakened from my sleep by a noise inside the wall of my bedroom. When I located the area of the noise, I saw a rat chewing and clawing through the wall. On another occasion, a rat chewed an electrical wire connected to an outlet, causing a small fire. It was not uncommon to hear about babies and children being bitten by rodents. If the lights were not left on at night, disease-carrying cockroaches would appear to move like a carpet when the light was turned on. Sometimes, it was frightening when they would crawl on you while sleeping. My landlord who lived in the northwest suburbs was not responsive to my request to send an exterminator to get rid of the rats and cockroaches.

Day Laborer Blues

I`m waiting in a (day labor) office up on Wilson
Just trying to find myself some work to do.
The man behind the counter says
Don't worry
"Cause there's work for every one of you"
And what he says is not true, Cause some of us won't be working
There's only ten or fifteen jobs to do.

— DOUG YOUNGBLOOD, DAY LABOR BLUES

"**H**illbillies! Most of my problem here is with the hillbillies. You can't rely on them. You send them out on a good three-week job, and for the first week they go great. They're good workers, most of them, but the second week they're gone, and there you are. Back to Tennessee to see if the fish are biting or wherever else they go. They just don't care," said Ray Holbrook, manager, Manpower Day Labor Agency.

People who had to leave their homeland contributed to what became known as the Migrant Circle. Southern migrants made their way into various cities throughout the north — Chicago, Detroit, Cincinnati, Cleveland and

Pittsburgh. Many migrants had to rely on jobs with unethical day-labor agencies. These jobs were usually unskilled, menial jobs that were physically demanding, and with a high risk of injury. Day labor agencies were not legally required to provide insurance because they were short-term contractors to the industry that needed the workers. Neither the agency nor the company provided any other benefits. Day laborers had no one to speak on their behalf, because they were not permanent employees, and therefore didn't qualify for any kind of union representation.

Laborers were always worried about whether they would be chosen for work the next day, and if the job would be safe. When an accident did occur, the worker would be dismissed without any kind of compensation. Injuries were treated by company-owned medical staff, usually a nurse. Major injuries were referred to local hospitals that gave only minimal treatment and discharged the worker. On so many occasions, an injured individual with handicapped conditions had no follow up visits, and hospitals eventually billed the patient due to a lack of insurance.

In 1966, "Southern whites" in Uptown exceeded the number of stable jobs in Chicago. Roger Guy attributed this to, "A low level of education and a lack of needed skills, combined with "Hillbilly" discrimination, increased the unemployment rate to 47% in Uptown. The national rate was only 3.8%." The lack of jobs in the North made it almost impossible for the Southern migrant to climb out of poverty. Those who were lucky enough to find stable employment would often send money, used clothing, and other items from resale stores to poor, Southern relatives to relieve some of their impoverished existence.

I worked as a day-laborer for a while, unloading trucks or as a janitor — mostly menial work that didn't require much skill. Most jobs involved back-breaking work, with only one ten-minute break and one half-hour lunch break on an eight-hour shift, that is if the employer decided to grant it. One man who had been working day-labor jobs for over two years told me: "If you wanted to be considered for work on a regular basis, you will eventually have to pay. You see, many of the people working in the office (day-labor agency) are on the take and will have you pay a percentage of what you make every day to guarantee you a job the next day. I have been giving them my money for a long time, but what can I do? I have to work because I can`t find no longtime job."

When I asked what can I do if they pay me by check, he said: "Then you will have to go next door to the currency exchange and pay them, and then give the office people their money. A lot of times they will give you cash and take out their part. I like it better that way, 'cause I don`t have to give the currency exchange people their part." That evening I was paid by check, and never returned to work for the day-labor office.

When Southerners failed to find jobs and a better way

of life in one city, they would either return back to "down home," or continue to another city. They also got the name "Midnight Movers," because most times a migrant would travel after dark to and from the South as cars didn't have air conditioning. The name was also applied to undocumented Latinos, because if they got word that the immigration authorities were near, they would move at night in order not to be noticed. The name was also applied to both groups, because if they did not have funds for rent, they would move out at night to escape payment.

Like evil twins, blood banks were often located next to day-labor agencies. Bank owners would target the poor for the purpose of purchasing their blood for resale to hospitals and other institutions in the medical field. For many desperate people, it was act of survival when there was little or no work at day-labor agencies. Families and individuals would calculate when it was safe and healthy for an adult to sell their blood, and for some families it was the only source of money that could be applied to their weekly earnings or government assistance to keep them fed and housed. I and several friends visited the blood banks on occasion to avoid hunger.

Poor people have always been described as lazy and not wanting to work by mainstream society. This is a false belief of ignorance that has permeated throughout history. One must look no further than the beginning of America, when England expelled its lower class and undesirables to the "New World." Once in the colonies, it did not take long for the English ruling class to use the poor as their servants, exploiting them as free or cheap labor. Anti-poor hatred has been catastrophic for poor people and has become a major belief by the mainstream society. It extends into every color and nationality. The Southern poor white did not escape the jaws of a monster that places them into a class of servitude, ignorance and worthlessness in today's society.

More generally within American culture at the time (and it is still the same now), many people believed that the poor are poor and uneducated because they want to be, and choose not to work. In fact, poverty and unemployment are problems caused by the capitalist exploitative economic system, and are not the fault of the individual. In her dissertation, my friend Colleen Wessel-McCoy said something that I agree with, about how we must explicitly identify the poor and poverty. She argues "against the idea that we must avoid language of 'poor' and 'poverty' because it is denigrating of human dignity, that we must challenge the idea that being poor is to be less human, and instead assert that an economy that creates poverty is what denigrates human dignity."

She further states that there is a need to reframe the identity of the poor "by focusing on the basic needs that are systematically denied: healthcare, education, debt, childcare, due process, the right to vote, freedom from mass incarceration, police violence, and reframe basic needs as unfulfilled human rights. To do so is to broaden the conversation about who is poor and what it means to be poor." The stereotype that Southern whites were lazy and did not want to work is just plain wrong. The city of Chicago did not have the resources, nor the desire, to provide for the needs of the poor of any color. Poor people were the product of a system that did not share the wealth, and did not invest in helping the poor out of poverty.

The poor Southerner has always struggled to make ends meet. Early settlers engaged in fur trading and bartering, while farming, to survive. The only saving grace and curse for some was when coal was found to be abundant in the Southern mountains, and mining was introduced in the 1700's. Mining was in full production in the 1870's, when railroads made it feasible to transport the coal. Still, many were subject to oppression and aggression by the coal company owners. Mining towns were created and required miners to live in cheap shacks. A company store was set up, and the miners had to purchase needed food and survival items at a price that was often several times more than the wages of the miners. In the 1890's, the miners had had enough abuse from the operators and joined the newly organized United Mine Workers Union, which was modeled after the American Federation of Labor that began years of pickets and strikes for better working conditions, medical benefits and wages.

In the early 1940's, many coal mines were shut down, due either to depletion or to coal operators refusing to cooperate with the unions. As Hollander and Gitlin described, "Between 1945 and 1965, the number of coal miners in the United States fell by three-quarters while productivity tripled. The total population of Southern Appalachia (West Virginia, eastern Kentucky, eastern Tennessee, North Carolina, some counties in north Georgia and north west Alabama) fell by 3.4 percent from 1950-1960 and the birth rate started falling in 1945."

Many people, especially well-to-do whites, could see the impacts of poverty, yet they ignored the cause by judging those who have little, without realizing that racism and classism overlap in a capitalist society. People of color are judged due to their skin color, and poor whites are looked down on as an inferior class of the white race. The poor and the wealthy see the world much differently.

Poor folks live in oppression and experience it in their lives on an hourly basis. Without seeing the true cause of poverty, it is impossible to understand poverty. It is like viewing poverty and judging the poor through one eye, because of what they lack materially, while keeping the other eye closed, which would reveal why the poor don't have what society determines as adequate. As long as we focus on the conditions of poverty and ignore its causes, we will never see the individual or group as having human value.

Chicago: City of Gangs, Mayor Daley Gang Leader

I n the 1960's, Chicago was very much a city of gangs. There were literally hundreds of different gangs. Every neighborhood had their own group of young people that stuck together, and saw themselves as protecting their area. There were Black and Latino gangs, and all sorts of different gangs of poor white people. It wasn't just people in poor neighborhoods that formed gangs. The city government itself was also essentially an elaborate and powerful gang.

Mayor Richard J. Daley was a product of a street gang, and ran the city as such. He knew the inner workings of street gangs, because his rise to power began in an Irish gang called the Hamburgs. The Hamburgs were his power base; they helped him stay in power for decades. Daley became one of the leaders of the Hamburgs, and this is where he got his first introduction to politics. First, the Hamburgs helped put Daley in the office of Sheriff of Cook County. Next, he was elected as a state representative, and then finally as mayor of Chicago. In exchange for his power, Daley repaid many members of the Hamburgs with high-ranking positions in Chicago's city government.

According to Daley, the Hamburgs were an "athletic" group. Hamburg members served a dual purpose for the Bridgeport community. On the one hand, they were streetwise when needed, keeping Blacks and other undesirables out of their Irish neighborhood. On the other, they were not afraid of physical confrontation if the occasion arose to defend their turf, but they were also clearly a political force when a political candidate benefited them.

Under Mayor Daley's leadership, and with many members of the Hamburgs working in the Chicago police department, they acted like a gang, harassing and terrorizing the poor whites and communities of color they patrolled. By police standards, the definition of gangs was any group that opposed the "Daley Machine." According to the City of Chicago, a gang was defined as three or more individuals gathered in one place, and they could be stopped and searched by the police for any reason.

There was also a time limit of fifteen minutes that an individual or group of people could stand in one location on the street. The search and seizure law was used excessively to stop vehicles without any cause and search them. If the cops determined that any occupant was guilty of a crime, or if drugs or weapons were found or planted by the cops, then the vehicle could be seized and impounded. Several vehicles were seized and never returned to the owner, without proof the owner was guilty of any wrongdoing.

Whenever the police wanted, they could order an individual to move, or a group to disband, under threat of facing arrest. Many times, there were no warnings. Several police officers would descend on a group of people with nightsticks or guns drawn, put them up against a wall or force them to lay on the sidewalk or street, and search them without any reason. It was also unwise for an individual to put a hand in their pocket, because the action would give the police the authority to either shoot, beat or arrest the individual. The cops would view it as being an attempt to retrieve a weapon. Many times, cops would use this as a justification, even if the individual did not make any attempt to put a hand in their pocket. Black Panther Stan McKenney told me that some leaders, such as Fred Hampton of the Illinois Black Panthers, would sew their pockets shut so the cops could not employee this technique.

There were many other tactics the police would use against street people or anyone that they identified as a problem. One tactic was to transport them to other areas of the city that had active gangs. A white person would be taken to a Black community and handed over to the police in that district, who would in turn drop the person off without any means of transportation. The cops would take their money and identification. Sometimes they would be beaten.

Females were not exempt from police harassment either. Mary Ellen Keniston, a member of the Young Patriots who worked with our Community Health Clinic was stopped while walking her dog in Uptown and transported to a Black, south side neighborhood. She was rescued by a Black woman, who gave her money for the train to return home. Both black and white communities knew that this was a police tactic and would assist their people to return home safely. The police still continued this tactic because they never knew, and were never concerned, with what happened to their victims.

Another favorite tactic of the Chicago Police was to open a thick Chicago phone-book or police helmet, place it over a person's head, and hit them repeatedly with a nightstick. It left no evidence of a physical beating, but gave the individual a headache or a concussion, and sometimes they were beaten unconscious. The 20th District police station in Uptown sported a bench with handcuffs on each end, so you couldn't dodge their punches as they beat the shit out of you. Another tactic to get a person to confess to a crime — combined with beating them — would be to deny them sleep during interrogation. After a long period of time, the person would usually confess, even though they did not commit any crime. This type of torture was very effective, whereby most individuals do not even realize they had confessed or signed a false confession.

According to Stan McKenny, a Black Panther member, "Cops have been known to cut out the finger nails of Black people in the Black community." They were also known to break fingers of poor whites as well.

The Daley Machine kept people in conflict using a perverse system of racism. The machine was very satisfied when gangs and ethnic and minority groups were fighting each other — that is, as long as the groups and gangs were in poor communities and did not cross the lines into middle or upper class white communities. If an older vehicle was spotted in any middle or upper class suburban neighborhood, they would be stopped, questioned and searched. Unless they had a reason for being there, they would be ordered to leave the neighborhood. Otherwise, they could be beaten or arrested. Often, domestic workers and those performing menial jobs were harassed and sometimes arrested for suspicious behavior.

Any person with a Southern accent was a target for the Chicago Police. Beatings and harassment were an everyday occurrence, and the cops showed no discrimination in age, gender, race or nationality. Native Americans, Hispanics and Blacks were also victims of police brutality. Police had ultimate authority to do whatever they deemed necessary to enforce what they believed to be the law.

What the Daley regime did not realize was that they were responsible for the creation of the many resistance organizations spawned by the oppressive, brutal and murderous system of repression which fostered interracial relationships and coalitions between poor Southern whites and people of color. As harassment continued, more and more people of all colors became convinced that if relief from oppression was ever to be achieved, it had to be fought on a local level, neighborhood by neighborhood.

It was absolutely vital that the fight had to be brought to the politicians and those who hold the key to the capitalist system, and to dispel their expectations that the poor would continue to be meek and subservient to elites. Even if it meant physical harm or imprisonment, it was time to organize, build coalitions, and set a firm foothold in neighborhoods to fight for self-determination from the suffocating Daley Machine.

Evolution of an Organizer

I n 1964, members of the Students for a Democratic Society (SDS) moved into Uptown to help the poor organize and control their community, calling themselves the "Jobs Or Income Now Community Union" (JOIN). SDS was a student organization that had grown out of an older socialist organization, the League for Industrial Democracy. One SDS co-founder, Tom Hayden, believed that society could be changed by an "interracial movement of the poor." He advocated that the poor should control their own lives and be educated on how to separate themselves from their oppressors. SDS recruited college students to live in poor communities, offering them knowledge and training in community organizing skills. Hayden, however, wrote in internal SDS reports, a statement that was soon to be proven wrong about the poor not being capable of organizing for their own self-determination:

Poor people know they are victimized from every direction. The facts of life always break through to expose the distance between American ideals and personal realities. This kind of knowledge, however, is kept undeveloped and unused because of another knowledge imposed on the poor, a keen sense of dependence on the oppressor. This is the source of universal fear which leads poor people to act and even think subserviently. Seeing themselves to blame for their situation, they rule out the possibility that they might be qualified to govern themselves and their organization. Besides fear, it is their sense of inadequacy and embarrassment which destroys the possibility of revolt.

Hayden's statement is only partially true. There are those who fear their oppressor and submit to them, much like a prisoner is forced to be subservient to the prison guard. But still, this was not representative of me or many of the community organizers that I met in Uptown. It was as though Hayden and some of the students believed that poor people were under some kind of hypnotic spell by their oppressor. What people like Hayden failed to understand is that poor people are expendable to their oppressor and that his statement perpetuates the belief that the oppressor is their superior.

In reality, the oppressed see the oppressor as being a lower form of human being and therefore not their superior, at least among the working and poor classes. But the oppressor can determine whether the poor can work and therefore feed themselves and their families. The force of the oppressors is a tremendous weight on the shoulders of the poor, especially the provider of the family. In many instances, there is no other alternative but to buckle under the oppressor's dictatorial conditions. This is called survival. But buckling under does not mean that the poor have accepted a position of servitude and shame. To the contrary, they only want to find an escape from their oppressor's control.

The student effort was initially funded by the United Workers Union through a project called the Economic Research and Action Project (ERAP), which had identified Uptown as needing assistance in finding jobs. ERAP consisted of ten projects in the United States, located in poor communities across the country. Through their research, they identified Uptown as having one of the highest unemployment rates in Chicago. Most of the students were Marxist and were surprised to learn that many of the Uptown poor were sympathetic to Marxist theory, but had never read or studied it. They did not know who Karl Marx was, or the definition of socialism. The students discovered a contradiction: Although the capitalist system had indoctrinated the poor that communism and socialism was bad for them, it wasn't hard to convince community residents that workers should have ownership of what they produced, and control over their futures.

Another thing that convinced the students who

came to the Southern white community was a directive from Black leaders, such as Stokely Carmichael from the Student Nonviolent Coordinating Committee telling white revolutionaries to "organize their own" to support the Black Freedom Movement. White students had been able to go into the deep South and participate in Freedom Summer and voter registration drives. Yet, Black organizers couldn't show up in white communities and start knocking on doors. Therefore, white people should be going into their own communities to fight racism. Uptown was a logical location to organize due to widespread racism in the community. The students who came to Uptown listened to Black leaders and tried to put the "organize your own" mandate into practice. This was not true of all of the ERAP projects. Some simply sent white students into Black northern communities.

The students rented a storefront in Uptown and offered their assistance in finding residents jobs. Soon, they realized that unemployment was only one issue facing the poor in Uptown: there was also police brutality and harassment, welfare rights, inadequate housing, absentee landlords, inadequate city services (such as garbage collection, street and sidewalk repair and cleaning), access to healthcare, and widespread poverty.

The first contact between the students and the poor of Uptown was a lukewarm endeavor. Outsiders were often viewed with suspicion. Communication was difficult because of cultural and educational differences. My first encounter with a student organizer was quite confusing. He used a lot of rhetoric like, "Power to the People," "Off the Pigs," "The streets belong to the people and not the Pigs," and quotations from the Red Book by Chairman Mao Zedong. I was also told by one student that country music was "just people feeling sorry for themselves." Country music was a very important part of the Southern culture and I considered the statement an insult.

For many students, this was their first contact with poor people. Some brought with them a great deal of middle-class values and behavior. But some developed a deep compassion for the poor. Some were first generation college students from working-class families and blended in better with the poor community residents. Still, there were a few who were naïve and believed the old myth that the poor could not develop their own leadership. To some residents, this idea seemed to contradict why student were organizing in the community and attempting to develop an indigenous leadership.

Because of the constant oppression from the Chicago city government and the police, residents were always in a state of rebellion, if not outright revolt. It was not until the 1960's that more residents began to organize community action groups that could not be controlled by the traditional Democratic Party, which historically kept their foot on the neck of organizations and individuals who advocated for social and economic change. SDS came to Uptown at a time that was ripe for community protests, and played a very instrumental role in offering structure to residents who were ready to lead and organize their community.

Many residents had been involved in coal mining confrontations, such as the Battle of Blair Mountain in Hazard County Kentucky during a union organizing drive that led to the murder of protesters at the hands of the company thugs, police and military. Many had knowledge of John Brown and Mother Jones. There was a long history of rebellion and friction between coal miners, as well as textile, agricultural and domestic workers, with unscrupulous and greedy company owners, such as Peabody Coal.

Jack (Junebug) Boykin, Bobby McGinnis, Ralph Thurman, Tom Melear, Sonny Broom, David Puckett and others gravitated to JOIN because of the organization's political rhetoric and the close proximity in age to the students. Boykin, McGinnis, Melear, Broom and Puckett were street leaders and organizers. Thurman had been a leader of the Peacemakers, a street gang made up of mostly Southern white youths. The gang`s history can be traced back to 1957, but the belief is that it originated just after World War II. Some of the members of this gang would become known as the Goodfellows, and later several members would organize the Young Patriots. Boykin and McGinnis were well respected by the street population, who considered them fair and good leaders.

JOIN student organizers like Mike James, Patrick Sturgis, Bob Lawson and others began hanging out with street guys, drinking in their bars, smoking weed and engaged them on police brutality and other issues that effected their everyday lives. Jobs were a major issue for JOIN, but police brutality was the primary reason for these streetwise individuals to associate with JOIN, because several of their friends had been murdered, beaten and jailed by the cops.

The Alpha Dog concept dominated the streets, and everyone understood who the leaders were. Some individuals were known as "peacemakers" or "peacekeepers," and they were entrusted to solve problems and settle conflicts by getting people to work out their differences. There could be more than one leader depending on which group the individual would hang out with. Some leaders were identified as the toughest when it came to defending their honor or turf. Respect was mutual between Southerners and non-Southerners, because they all understood that they share the same oppressive conditions.

The term "street people" came to identify the people who hung out on the street and developed a bond of brotherhood and sisterhood. Outsiders, such as students, could be an affiliate or sometimes engage in illegal activities and events, but would not be considered a full member of the group. One had to earn their place in the group and be representative of the culture, socioeconomic status, and sometime the toughness of the individual. This structure made it much easier to organize, recruit and get support when it became necessary.

Female students also found a more secure bond with the neighborhood women. Diane Fager, Nancy Hollander, Marilyn Katz, Nora Davis, and Pam Grey found favor with community residents, including Mary Hockenberry, Candace Hockenberry, Dovie Thurman, Dovie Coleman, Peggy Terry, and Kit Komatsu, a Civil Rights Movement Freedom Rider. Through these friendships, JOIN organized survival programs, such as food coops, welfare unions, community theatre, and many other programs that directly improved the lives of uptown residents. They also organized rent strikes, boycotts of businesses, and took over and managed a building in Uptown. Their newspaper, the "Firing Line," educated the community by addressing issues of liberation struggles, such as women's rights, civil rights, and the anti-war movement, as well as news of liberation movements in developing countries.

The history of the Chicago police has always been one of corruption. The cops in Uptown were from the 20th District, and in 1959 they were involved in the famous "Summerdale Scandal" that led to the conviction of eight officers and the removal of Police Commissioner Timothy O'Conner. After this humiliation, it changed its name to the Foster Avenue District, the street where it was located. In 1958, a 20th District detective named Frank Faraci stopped Richard Morrison, a well-known burglar, and forced him to be his personal burglar. Morrison would fill a shopping list from Faraci and his cop buddies for personal use and resale. But the heists came to an end when another cop, who was unaware of the scheme, arrested Morrison with stolen merchandise. After hearing Morrison's story, the cop was given immunity for turning state's evidence against Faraci and his band of thieves.

After much embarrassment, Mayor Richard J. Daley brought in police reformer Orlando Winfield Wilson as Superintendent of Police. Wilson had served as Chief of Police in Fullerton, California and Wichita, Kansas, and was the author of several books on policing and police techniques. He was tasked with reorganizing the Chicago Police Department to get it out from the stigma as being corrupt and controlled by politicians, crime syndicates, and city officials.

Wilson taught that the police had little control over social causes, such as poverty and neglect, and discouraged officers from getting personally involved with residents. However, police could repress and control crime through aggressive tactics, such as preventative mobile patrols. He believed that police using police vehicles had a better chance of solving, deterring and preventing crime as well as arresting law breakers, because cops would still be able to observe, talk to, and interact with community residents. Wilson did not foresee cops remaining in their vehicles for most of their shift and consequently becoming isolated from the public.

There had always been a disrespect by the police toward the poor in minority communities due to segregation, in addition to class differences. There was already little trust between locals and the police, and due to cops being transferred in and out of the communities, officers saw no need in being friends with community residents they did not know or respect. Soon cops began to apply more force, and found it more convenient to transport arrestees to the local police station. Both cops and residents began to view each other as enemies.

If Wilson wanted to deter crime, his plan failed miserably. Due to all cops having more mobility, it became easier to transfer them to all parts of the city. This became evident when bad cops were being transferred in and out of poor communities. Many of the officers were misfits, and had little to no respect for the neighborhood they were patrolling. Some had a reputation for being psychotic and unstable. These communities would be a perfect place to assign these undesirable cops. It was a perfect plan, because the poor were considered an undesirable population.

It did not take long for Wilson to become a memory after his departure from Chicago. Daley used Wilson's great reforms to praise Chicago's finest. The mayor again appointed his machine pawns to increase his wrath on those who opposed him and to carry out his policies of oppressing the poor. Police brutality, graft and murder by the cops increased. Again, it was business as usual. Patronage increased and syndicate ties were once again restored. The new police force became the same old police force.

In the late 60's and through the 70's, the cops had a "safe house" in the 47th Democratic Precinct, west of Uptown, where they would take prostitutes and other women to be sexually victimized. The highest-ranking police officer that I knew to use the location was a police lieutenant, and the person allowing its use was a Democratic precinct captain. An incident of cops raping a young woman there has been documented in the book, "Uptown, Poor Whites in Chicago," after a woman came to the JOIN office and reported the crime to the staff. I have witnessed cops whistling and making sexual remarks to women, even when their children and husbands were present.

By looking at Mayor Daley's behavior toward the poor, one could come to the conclusion that he didn't care if corruption and oppression occurred. With his statement that there are "no slums in Chicago," he had attempted to make slums invisible to those who had no contact with the poor in his city. Many believed his lies, and yet he needed the poor neighborhoods to compile crime statistics in order to request state and federal funds for the police and other city programs. The police were also used as a tool to aggravate tensions between gangs and poor residents, encouraging violence between them. His police gang was a major contributor to violence, rape, extortion and murder in poor communities.

My first of many encounters with the Chicago Police was during my second week in Uptown in March, 1967. While walking down Sunnyside Avenue, two uniformed cops stopped me, handcuffed me, and put me in the back seat of their patrol car, accusing me of burglarizing apartments in the neighborhood. I felt as though I was reliving the false accusations against me in my hometown by the local cops. I explained that I had no idea what they were talking about. And then one of them asked if I knew anyone who had been committing burglaries in the neighborhood. I informed them that I did not.

One of the cops asked for my identification, and I could only show my Social Security card. He asked to see my Selective Service card. I informed him that I was only seventeen, and could not register until I was eighteen. He then asked me if I wanted to buy an ID card? When I did not buy the ID, he became very angry and said: "Just another fucking hillbilly! All you hillbillies are stupid and we don't want you here! Just go back from where you come from and fuck your mother, sister, brother, dog or whoever you people fuck down there. Now get the fuck out of my car! If I see you again, I won't be so nice."

At that point, one cop pulled me from the car, pushed

my face first to the ground, and placed his foot on the side of my head while the other cop uncuffed me, still cursing me. It was this behavior that convinced me that I could never trust a Chicago cop.

In June 1967, a woman called the JOIN office and reported that she was having a dispute with her landlord on Kenmore Avenue. She said he was in the process of throwing their clothes into the street and would not allow her back into the building, because she was going to inform his wife that he was making sexual advancements toward her.

When Mike James, Sonny Nevell and I arrived, the tenant, landlord and two of his relatives were having a heated argument. She claimed that she had paid her rent, but he wanted her out before she could talk with his wife. The tenant said she called the cops, who only drove by and did not stop. The landlord ordered us off his property and asked his relatives to call the cops. This time the cops did stop, heard both sides, and sided with the landlord, even though the tenant had a paid rent receipt. The cops claimed that because she did not have a lease, the landlord can legally evict her.

We informed the landlord that a JOIN lawyer would represent her if she chose to file harassment charges, which made him angry and came toward us. Mike James was the closest, so he extended his arm to stop the landlord. The cops did not like JOIN and that gave them the opportunity to arrest us three on assault and disorderly conduct charges, and they hauled us off to the Summerdale Police Station. In August, we were found guilty on the disorderly conduct charge, while the assault charge was dismissed.

The Chicago Police were always keeping an eye on organizations that worked with street guys, the homeless, or those who they determined to be undesirables. There was an organization active in the area called the Friendship House, which was sponsored by the Reverend George Morey from the United Presbyterian Church. Reverend Morey would give the street guys a place to get off the street and play pool, play their musical instruments, or just sit and talk. He would also try to find jobs for them. The center he ran was often visited by the Community Relations Officer from the Summerdale Police station. Reverend Morey was trying to find me a job when the Community Relations Officer came in and said that he was interested in helping me and that he knew a place that had an opening. He would check it out and see me the next day.

Morey told me that he didn't trust the cops, but that there weren't many jobs available, encouraging me to check it out. He feared that the cops would want something in return, because it was not in their nature to help the people of Uptown. We agreed that since I did not have a job, I should accept the offer. The cop arranged for an interview with Central Watch at the Wells Fargo Company, which monitored security alarms for business and residential customers.

The interviewer said that he did not have open positions but was creating one because he and the sergeant were friends. I was given a polygraph test, but no questions of significance were asked — just name, age, address and birthdate. I started to work the next day from 11pm until 7am. The job consisted of sitting at a workstation and reporting any breach in a security system, i.e. when someone had entered a business or residence without disarming the alarm. In the end, I never had the opportunity to actually carry my duties, because I received no training and, in any case, someone else monitored my station. All I did was sit at my station and sleep most of the time.

One morning, after about three weeks of being on the job, and as I was ending my shift, the sergeant and another man in a suit picked me up in an unmarked police car and wanted to take me to breakfast. The suited man said that I was doing an excellent job, and that he had talked to his boss and they had big plans for me. Then, he got to why they wanted to talk to me. He said that I was an intelligent guy, and that they wanted to provide a better life for me. All I had to do was to work for them. They wanted me to keep them informed about any plans by the Peacemakers, JOIN, SDS, Reverend Morey, and any other radical organizations that I come in contact with.

I had knots in my stomach and felt like throwing up. They wanted me to be an informant against the only friends that I had. I was one of the guys. I wanted to improve my conditions, but I could not turn against my people. I had been harassed by cops in my hometown and Chicago and had seen police brutality against the people of Uptown. I told them that I would not accept their offer. Of course, they told me how ungrateful I was and said that I need not return to work. I often wondered if the cops and the FBI had arrangements with other businesses to lure people into becoming informants. At that moment, I made a commitment to better myself by working against the oppressive capitalist system and serve the people. I became more involved in the community.

Marching on Summerdale

The sun is setting in the sky.
The color of red like the blood of dying
They've beaten us down till we're almost crying.
Gotta do something or die tryin'
Guys been scared to long, too long,
Scared of the blue lights flashing wrong.
Been slapped enough to bleed to dawn,
Getting together and singing this song.
They call us punks and jerks and bums,
Call us dumb, stumper — Jumpers, hillbillies
Tell us to go back to where we came from
If we've done nothing they make up a tale.
We ain't got nothing to make our bail.
That's why we are marching on Summerdale.

n August of 1966, around 250 former Peacemakers and members of JOIN and community residents (including Native Americans and Latinos) marched on the Summerdale police station demanding an end to police brutality and murder by the police. The protesters specifically called for the firing of a notorious bad cop named Sam Joseph, who was known for his dislike of the street guys and his brutal tactics on community residents, as well as the creation of a civilian review board to monitor police behavior.

The cops countered the march by recruiting a group called the Dover Boys, who were from the west side of Uptown, and were better off economically, with family ties to the Democratic Party. They and other friends of the cops taunted the protesters. Cops would look the other way while the Dovers raced their cars through Uptown and Lake Michigan's Lakefront.

When the protesters arrived at the Summerdale station, they were greeted by Detective Sam Joseph, who informed them that he was "going to kill every fucking one of you." Bob Lawson was threatened again several days later by the same detective who told him, "We are going to march all over your head."

Detective Joseph had a very checkered history of mistreating people. He was also the most decorated cop in Chicago. One would think that with all his commendations that he would be commanding his own district, or given a cushy office downtown. So, why was he stuck in Uptown? Because cops, particularly those that were misfits and psychotic, were placed in poor communities in Chicago. Who in Daley's administration cared if the poor were beaten?

Joseph had overstepped his boundaries in 1965, when he severely beat a middle-class kid. Charges were brought against him, and the Internal Investigation Division (IID) recommended he be suspended for thirty days. But he was untouchable. In response, several politicians called for the IID itself to be investigated.

The civilian review board that the protesters were demanding never materialized, but the beatings, arrests and harassment continued. Sam Joseph became more blatant and brutal, especially against those who were identified as instigators on the march by the Chicago Police Gang Intelligence Unit, whose duties were to identify and investigate gang members (while the Red Squad would monitor those individuals and groups that were considered a threat to Chicago or the federal government, and might have unpatriotic beliefs).

In September, as a retaliation for the Foster Avenue march, narcotics agents from the Chicago Police Department and the State of Illinois Police raided the JOIN office and the office of the United Presbyterian Church, after they had broken in and planted the drugs. Two JOIN organizers, Reverend George Morey, and two bystanders were arrested and charged with possession of drugs. Both offices were almost totally destroyed. Several months later, all charges were dropped.

The night following the raid, the Chicago cops killed Danny Williams, brother of an active Goodfellow. Many stories have been told about the killing. But the one most repeated is that Williams was known as a fighter with a quick temper. On this particular day, he was stopped by two cops who had history with him and disliked him. An argument ensued, and he began to run. The cops shot him in the back and killed him. Some stories have it that he was told to leave by the cops, and then they shot him. Regardless of which story is true, JOIN student organizer Bob Lawson states, "Even though Williams was a rough guy, the cops could have wounded him, and he did not deserve to die like that."

A week later, about twenty-five community residents and Good Fellows held a memorial service for Williams at Broadway and Wilson, the site of the murder. As usual, the cops surrounded the gathering and broke up the service, based on anti-loitering law that makes it illegal for more than three individuals to occupy the same location for over fifteen minutes without a permit. The cops were afraid that if the crowd was to grow any bigger, they would not be able to control them, giving the protesters an opportunity to draw more residents to the protest.

Two weeks later, Michael Alcanter, a young Native American who attended the march, was severely beaten by cops. In particular, he was known to be on Detective Joseph's enemy list. This song from "Uptown: Poor Whites in Chicago," by my brother Ralph Thurman tells what happened to Michael:

It was late one night, the cops were riding round
Looking for someone to stomp into the ground
When just as they passed
A little boy threw a glass
They stopped but they did not hear a sound.

They remembered Michael from some time ago,
He was fast asleep so he didn't know.
Two policemen came inside
And turned on all the lights
They grabbed him and said let's go.
As they opened the door that led into the street
They shoved him and he fell to his feet.
And when he turned around
They knocked him to the ground.
They hit him till his head began to bleed

By this time another policeman joined the fun.
He tried to get up but he was nearly done.
I could tell he was in pain
But they kicked him just the same
Michael pleaded but they kept on with their fun.

Still they beat him with their clubs and fists and feet.
Michael was helpless as he lay there on the street.
Plenty of people were on hand
But no one would give a hand
As poor Michael just lay there in the street

I wonder what the world's coming to
You can't even trust the man in the blue.
I'm sure the man above
Didn't mean this to be love
If he did then it's not right for me and you.

In September of 1966, the Good Fellows and JOIN organizers marched on Chicago City Hall demanding still an end to police brutality and a citizen's review board to investigate and stop the Summerdale Police District from "framing, beating and killing people they don't like." Also, they wanted "city funds, so all the people in Uptown can have decent apartments and low rents, and welfare recipients to get more money and be treated like human beings." Our flyer stated: "Mayor Daley and other big shots don't know what it's like to live in Uptown — they don't even care! So why should they boss us around and make it hard on us." Again, their demands fell on deaf ears, and the cops retaliated with their abusive victimization on the people.

Early in 1967, the Good Fellows and JOIN organized a police watch committee modeled after the Black Panther

Party's "Police Patrols" in Oakland, California. Their purpose was to go out into the community to monitor and document suspicious and illegal activities by the police. JOIN activists Nancy Hollander, Bob Lawson and Ralph Thurman would be the first to conduct a "police patrol." On the first night, they witnessed two cops beating an unarmed man. Lawson asked the cops why they were doing this, and was given no explanation and told "to stay out of this."

After the cops discovered that they were being photographed, they confiscated a camera from Hollander. The activist had agreed that if anyone attempted to confiscate the camera, Thurman would run with it to a secure location. Hollander would then give up an old Brownie camera instead. The cops destroyed the film and camera, believing that they were getting rid of the evidence. Lawson protested the action, and was arrested and later released. The photos were used to prove police brutality by printing them on flyers and in the JOIN newspaper, "The Firing Line."

Standing On Our Own

n 1968, local community leaders asked SDS and other outsiders to leave JOIN. Conflicts arose between the two and charges of elitism arose against some of the students. Some community leaders felt that they were being "mother-henned" by the student organizers, and that they had grown in their knowledge and organizing skills to "organize on their own."

Peggy Terry wrote in a statement for the Uptown Poor People`s Coalition, "Through a deep and sometimes painful analysis and self-examination, it was decided to build our own organization and movement on the perspective of poor and working people organizing their own people and community. We of JOIN Community Union understand now that freedom and human dignity cannot be won for poor whites unless and until it is won for all exploited people."

Some community participants felt that some of the students were not allowing community residents control over major decisions that they believed were best for the community. The community felt that some students were more interested in international revolution and the anti-draft movement than the needs of the community, or that they were there for an adventure and were unwilling to make a commitment for the long haul. Bobby McGinnis and Peggy Terry led the charge. But a different, more positive, relationship and respect did develop with those who made a commitment to stay in the community and listen to its suggestions and plans.

The student leaders, for their part, believed that the job of an organizer was to work themselves out of a job, and allow the community leadership to have control of their own destiny. A major point of contention was when Rennie Davis, an SDS leader and anti-war advocate and organizer, overruled a request by the community leaders that they organize a rent strike in a building. This was an example of the JOIN leadership's reluctance to accept the community's demands to take action against that "urban renewal" that had targeted Uptown.

Class and cultural differences were a source of tension between most students and residents. Some community people felt that many students had the opportunity to return to their middle-class homes when it suited them, and some had already left to work on the national anti-war movement. The students were not disliked, but the cultural and economic differences played a role in keeping them from being fully accepted.

The belief was that some students had a concern about the plight of the poor, but they could not relate because they had not experienced long-term poverty. They were also looked upon as having the education and resources to enter into long-term careers and therefore retain their middle-class status by wealth being handed down to them for generations. When, for instance, living in dilapidated roach and rat-infested buildings became intolerable, the student would often times leave Uptown to live in a more suitable neighborhood, move to another state, or return home.

Community members believed that student organizers had the luxury of building a counterculture movement, and whenever they decided could fit in with mainstream society. The community organizers were attempting to get the students to understand that the poor community residents have been rejected by mainstream society. In addition, most Uptown people had not been exposed to the radical left movement, and did not understand what the movement was trying to accomplish. Students were viewed as long-haired hippies protesting the Vietnam War and using drugs.

There were additional charges by the community that were never addressed. Strong pressure to expel the students came from community women, who felt that their "men" were being influenced by some of the female students through friendships or sexual contacts. Underlying jealousies grew that should have been addressed. Students were also viewed as outsiders and distrusted by street people who were not a part of JOIN.

Uptown's streets were not a safe place for the students, and many felt that they could not understand their culture and street survival. To understand the crimes committed on the streets, one needed to understand the cause of poverty and brutality that existed on an everyday basis. Lack of education and opportunities, as well as class hatred, played a major role in committing crimes to exist or face starvation. Many turned to alcohol that ruined their lives. Pool hustlers, pimps, prostitutes, drugs, stolen property, gambling, robbery, violence — all played a major role in one's survival. Very seldom would students visit the pool halls and bars without the accompaniment of a community resident. They were not street trustworthy.

After the JOIN split, many student organizers stayed in Chicago and organized much needed services to the people. Rennie Davis was arrested and charged with inciting a riot during the 1968 Democratic Convention, along with the seven others who came to be called the "Chicago Eight." Marilyn Katz was instrumental in organizing the Chicago Women's Liberation Movement. Diane Fager, Bob Lawson, Norrie Davis and others helped organize Rising Up Angry with Mike James. Rising Up Angry was similar in spirit to the Young Patriots. They attempted to organize white gang-affiliated youth, known at the time as Greasers.

In its 5-year history, JOIN convinced residents to fight for their community. It taught "participatory democracy," formed tenant unions, helped to organize a march against police brutality, built food co-ops, formed a People's Theatre, engaged in the war on poverty, helped perform lead screening drives, and held community rallies, picnics, and demonstrations at the welfare office and city hall. They helped win a fight to get a children's playground on Clifton Avenue for the benefit of all Uptown residents.

Many community residents had become members of JOIN and participated in community projects. They supported Mike James, who led the rally for the Good Fellows to continue their development of organizational skills. Several students who moved into Uptown were accepted by the Patriots. Mary Ellen and Andy Keniston, who were from working class families, moved from Ohio after hearing of us. They were able to ease the suspicion of outsiders with Southern families.

At the time of the JOIN split, I was new to the community and organizing. Now, and in retrospect, I feel that it was not a good decision to ask the students to leave Uptown, because many had developed strong friendships and were distressed that the community would ask them to leave after all their efforts to help the poor to organize and fight. More time should have been dedicated to working out our differences. Perhaps more debate on how their exodus would leave the community vulnerable. The students provided much needed numbers at protests and events. Their activism had taught the community many organizing techniques.

Some students felt that they had become a part of the community, and considered it unfair to select some to stay and others to leave. Other means to unify the students and community could have been instituted. This was a bond that need not to have been broken. In an interview with Paul Seigel, Peggy Terry stated, "It was the worst political mistake of my life throwing the students out." It wasn't until I became a student and college graduate that I could understand the students' thinking and behavior. It would be beneficial to have another student movement in the US, where students and community could work together.

Change comes hard for some. I witnessed the difficulty of change within my own family. Soon after my graduation from college, I noticed that several family members began to treat me as if I didn't understand them. They believed that I had changed so much that I no longer fit in with the family. Some thought that I was above my raising. Some relatives avoided me at family gatherings, or if I met them in public. All were polite, but I knew there was a stress on our relationship. I was given the nickname "professor." I thought back on how I had viewed the college students as being when we first met.

Organizing in the Aftermath

After the JOIN split, one of the first projects was to organize the National Community Union (NCU), an effort to bring the poor and factory workers across America together. The NCU decided to run Peggy Terry for vice president through the Peace and Freedom Party in California, with Eldridge Cleaver of the Black Panther Party as the presidential candidate. Their opponents were George Wallace, Richard Nixon and Hubert Humphrey, all of whom were also running for president. Mike James became their campaign manager.

Both Cleaver and Terry were most interested in confronting Governor Wallace of Alabama on his views about racism, segregation and white supremacy, and to expose class and racial hatred in the United States. Further, Cleaver and Terry attempted to educate the public that there was little difference in the living conditions of poor whites and poor Blacks, and that they needed to use this commonality to unite and organize with each other. They did not win the election, or personally confront George Wallace, but they did manage to spread the idea that Blacks and whites could unite to fight for freedom. The campaign proved that Blacks and poor Southern whites could overcome their divisions by years of segregation, and that the baton of racism and hate does not have to be handed on to future generations.

Another logical step forward for the new JOIN was to participate in the Southern Christian Leadership Conference's (SCLC) Poor People's Campaign, which was led by Martin Luther King Jr. and was to take place in Washington DC with the aim of bringing together poor people of all colors across the US. I was very excited to attend the campaign, because I followed everything that Dr. King did and said. On December 4, 1967, Dr. King announced the Poor People's Campaign and a march on Washington DC to make the world and politicians aware of the plight of the poor. I was very much impressed with Dr King`s move from civil rights to class struggle. Sadly, Dr. King did not get a chance to see his dream, because on April 4, 1968, he was murdered in Memphis, Tennessee. But his dream lived on when Ralph Abernathy took over at the SCLC, and decided to continue the Poor People's Campaign.

In May of 1968, a group from JOIN, Good Fellows and the Native American Committee left from Uptown to Washington DC to take up residence at Resurrection City. But it was a disastrous trip by bus. On our journey, we stopped to pick up other attendees and food in Ohio. The food had been poisoned. Many of us got very sick and were put up by volunteers and other concerned people. After a few days of recuperating, Junebug Boykin and I joined Peggy Terry, Doug Youngblood, Carol Blakely, Earl Hess, Mark Steiner, Tom Livingston, Guy Carawan and Pet Seeger in our tent village.

We were assigned plywood huts with four to a hut. It was exhilarating to be with thousands of people who came to protest economic injustice, racism and classism. We attended the rally meetings and made many friends. Perhaps one of the most enjoyable moments was when we sat around a campfire listening to, and singing with, legends like Pete Seeger, Guy Carawan and others. I lived in Tent City for two weeks. The only drawback was the constant rain. I was more wet than dry. There were some reports that the government was seeding the clouds to make it rain on us. At times, I believed that to be true. The other concern was that every time we would leave the park, we would be stopped by the Park Police and some-times detained, while background checks were conducted. It was an amazing trip, and I would do it again should there be another Resurrection City.

Good Fellows in the Community

I n 1968, myself, Junebug Boykin and Bobby Joe McGinnis of the Good Fellows were growing increasingly more political, due to the Civil Rights Movement, the anti-war movement, and revolutions and social unrest in other countries. We were becoming more frustrated with issues facing our community. Both Boykin and McGinnis were young associates of the Peacemakers and the Good Fellows. Boykin and his family had migrated from Tennessee, while McGinnis and his family came from Georgia. Both were children when they arrived in Chicago, and both had been victims of the harsh treatment by the cops and living in Uptown. Both were members of JOIN, where they learned how to organize groups to fight the system and demand their rights. They took me into their group when I first arrived in Uptown in 1967. They were my mentors and

I owe them a debt that I can never repay, particularly for their patience in introducing me to radical politics.

Community groups were splintered and competing for membership. Hunger, poverty, police brutality, sickness and medical needs continued to plague the community. The Urban Renewal Program would displace thousands of poor residents, and the Model Cities War on Poverty program was losing the war, because Mayor Daley controlled all aspects of the program, and he was not known for compassion for the poor. City organized committees did not represent the poor. The poor could not sit on the urban renewal committees, because they were not land owners, nor did the Model Cities Advisory Committee have any power in the decision-making process. Suggestions by the community and organizations would be heard at one meeting, only to be ignored or unrecognized at the next. The Mayor had final approval of all decisions. The Committees were nothing more than window dressing for city government.

The War on Poverty Program created by President Lyndon Johnson in 1966 provided federal funds to improve the lives of the poor, by attempting to offer much-needed services to poor communities. Woodlawn, Grand Boulevard, Lawndale and Uptown were chosen to receive funds. Chicago neighborhoods were chosen to receive funds for a variety of social service programs. The plan was a major failure, because the Johnson administration and Congress thought that bigger government was necessary and should control the program.

So, a web of agencies and departments were set up within cities that were to receive federal financing. All funds were to be controlled by the Office of Economic Opportunity, which itself was a maze of bureaucracy. Most funds were directed to Urban Progress Centers (UPC) set up in recipient cities to determine a particular neighborhood's needs. Given that Chicago city government is notoriously corrupt, Daley demanded that any federal money coming into his city should be controlled by his administration, or he would not participate in the program.

In the end, Daley won. He began placing administrators and staff who were dedicated to his machine to run the UPC. Neighborhood residents were hired and placed in menial positions. When it came time for elections, they would have to bring in the vote from constituents they served, such as senior citizens, handicapped (mental and physical), or those receiving food and other services. If they did not perform, they did not work. Most workers had to be recommended by a Democratic precinct captain or a ward committeeman to verify their party commitment.

The same system would hold true for the Urban Renewal Program (URP). The URP, or what would come to be called the "poor people's removal program," was a federal program in the Department of Housing and Urban

Development (HUD) that funded the demolition of old dilapidated structures and buildings in urban cities. The eminent domain law was put into effect to allow the purchase of private property for public use.

Initiated by a group of wealthy middle-class residents, Uptown's urban renewal plan began in 1955 along the lakefront, which formed the eastern boundaries of Uptown stretching along the shores of Lake Michigan. The Uptown Chicago Commission (UCC) was established, and all members were appointed by Mayor Daley. The UCC would oversee all urban renewal plans for Uptown. Of course, not one poor Uptown resident was allowed to participate.

The community came together to fight the Urban Renewal Program, and the Good Fellows were a part of it. A Poor People's Coalition was organized to prevent their homes from being demolished. The Poor People's Statement read as follows:

We, the poor unrepresented peoples of Uptown ... in the years we have lived here in Uptown,
Have heard the city government say, "We represent you"
We have heard the state government say, "We represent you"
We have heard the federal government say, "We represent you"
But — we are still unrepresented.
We have heard the city say, "We will help you"
We have heard it from the federal government and the poverty programs.

Now we hear it from Model Cities.
But we are still poor.
Before we came here, we lived on farms or in other cities.
We lived in Appalachia, or Indian Reservations, or on the south and west side of Chicago, or in Puerto Rico, Mexico and Cuba.
We left our homes there because life was hard, and we came here looking for something better… for something of our own.

The Good Fellows and the Poor People's Coalition had had enough of the Commission`s lies and deceit. The maintained that the UCC was engaged in displaying class hatred, and the poor would not tolerate it anymore. Now, the UCC would have to listen to our demands. As a result, many meetings were disrupted, and their plans were tabled until their next meeting.

The Good Fellows began by lending support to other groups in the community: the Voice of the People (which worked on tenant-landlord issues), the Native American Committee, the American Indian Center, JOIN, and other organizations. The Good Fellows let the other organizations know that they could work together, but would not join their organization and remain autonomous. They wanted to make their own decisions regarding issues and programs, without relying on the opinions and decisions of other organizations, activist or adults.

Some organizations wanted us to show up at their meetings only to exclude us from the decision-making process. Most adults felt that we were too young to make decisions for the community, although our life experience proved the opposite. Ranging in age from 15 to 21, most of us had never known a childhood due to having to work hard for most of our youth. Many of us also survived a harsh street life, while being victimized by police brutality and poverty. Adult decisions had to be made at an early age. The needs of the community were clear to us, and we were not willing to sit through hours of discussions to find solutions. We were ready to organize our own way and control our destiny.

The War in the Neighborhood and The Birth of the Young Patriots

The community still thought of us as members of the Good Fellows, whose past accomplishments were the march on the Summerdale Police Station and police monitoring. Many of the Peacemakers and older members had either moved back South or got drafted to the Vietnam War. Several of us had become more political in left-wing ideology and politics, seeing ourselves more as revolutionaries, and therefore needed a more appropriate name. In the history of the American Revolutionary War, the "Patriot" was someone who fought to liberate people from the oppressive government of England. So, we decided on the name "Young Patriots Organization."

The Patriots wanted the people to be liberated. We defined liberation as people having the freedom and power to make their own decisions concerning their lives, free from the threats and tyranny of an oppressive government that controlled their existence. We wanted to help the people regain the dignity that had been taken from them.

The message that we were relating to the community had to be very clear and in the language that they understood. We avoided intellectual and philosophical discussions to keep them from moving to the other side of the street when they saw us. Our Southern dialect and street knowledge allowed us to have identification with them and share the same culture. They could relate to us, because we shared the same living conditions and experiences that life had forced on them.

As a group, the Patriots were able to articulate the meaning of class hatred, economic oppression and racism, and tried to convince the community that their participation in direct action could bring about change in their lives. But some did not want to look to the future and had given up on a better life. We set out to convince them that it was worth working for a world where oppressive conditions could be overcome.

We were angry and determined not to become disillusioned, and to continue to fight the hard fight. We were willing to pick up the gun, if necessary, to defend our community. The more we organized and showed up at community meetings, the more residents began to respect us. If the city and programs like the War on Poverty and Urban Renewal were not going to recognize the needs of the community, then we would put them into effect ourselves and make them recognize us.

The Patriots were committed to fight Daley and his "poor people's removal program" to the end. Judging from past history, we knew that educational institutions and upper-class housing development were favorites of Daley as excuses to drive the poor out of their communities in the past. In the 1950's, fifty million dollars in state and federal funds were used to build the University of Chicago in the Hyde Park neighborhood, removing poor Italians, Mexicans, and Blacks, without replacing the housing that was destroyed. Instead, the city built housing that the poor could not afford, turning the Hyde Park neighborhood into an upper- and middle-class community. The same thing happened in Lincoln Park when the Carl Sandberg Village was built, driving out poor Puerto Ricans who were already pushed out of other neighborhoods.

Uptown was not exempt from Chicago's removal plan. The fight between Uptown's poor community and the City of Chicago intensified when Daley created the Uptown Conservation Community Council (UCCC), loading it with business owners and supporters from the Lakefront. Five community residents representing the poor applied for membership: Chuck Geary, manager of the

Tri-Faith Employment Agency and director of the Uptown Area People's Planning Committee; James Osborn, owner of the Book Box bookstore and community organizer for the United Presbyterian Church (and a member of the Young Patriots); Tina Resa, community resident and day-care worker; Emily Eaton, community resident; and Peggy Terry, community organizer and editor of the Firing Line newspaper, as well as former vice presidential candidate. All were rejected because none of them owned residential property. Osborn argued that he was a business owner and should be allowed a seat on the committee. He pointed out that while other committee members owned businesses in Uptown, their residential properties were in other areas. Osborne was railroaded because Mayor Daley would not recognize his request.

The Daley administration announced plans to build a community college in Uptown, and the UCCC welcomed it with great enthusiasm. The council members loved the idea that urban renewal might re-establish these areas as middle-class communities. The UCCC believed that building the community college would force out the poor, allowing the council to restore economic stability to their community. The area that was chosen for the college was 11.5 acres, and would displace 1,200 low-income apartments.

In 1969, the Young Patriots offered their support to the new Uptown Area People's Planning Coalition, which was made up of several organizations to protest the location and building of the college. The coalition brought in older Volunteers in Service to America volunteers Rodney and Sydney Wright, who were also architects. The Wrights had built the first solar community in Wisconsin and donated their time. The project proposed by the coalition was named the "People's Village," but later changed to the "Hank Williams Village," due to a large number of Southerners that would be displaced by the college.

The People's Proposal

The Hank Williams Village was designed as a Southern town. The plan sought to rehabilitate housing structures that could be saved, and build new housing units in the location of buildings that had to be destroyed. It would meet the needs of the poor and working class by offering low-income housing with a cul-de-sac plan and ample parking. The plan displayed some individual homes and condominiums, and proposed ideas about securing loans for those who could eventually buy a permanent home.

Services would be available through a pharmacy, legal services, park and recreational playground, co-operative food program, laundry facilities, employment services, and a hotel for new arrivals. A Village Hall would serve as a community meeting place, and administer collection of rent. Further, the coalition proposed alternative sites in north Uptown and the old Riverview Amusement Park, which had been vacant for many years. Both sites were denied, because the location was too far north, and the owners of Riverview wanted to develop businesses there.

Planning for the Hank Williams Village involved residents who lived in the geographical area. It would be located in the area bounded by Montrose on the south, Beacon on the West, Wilson on the North, and the L tracks parallel to Broadway on the east.

The Village was intended to meet the specific needs of Uptown residents. It would provide low income housing while also being an economically integrated community. It was intended to be a cooperative community, it will provide services which would be economically and socially beneficial to all residents, and which at the same time will serve to bind people together in a feeling of mutual responsibility and mutual advantage.

The original proposal of the Voice of the People organization to the Uptown Conservation Community Council outlined our belief in self-government.

And the Hank Williams Village is intended to meet the needs for citizens in neighborhood government. It is, to the best of our knowledge, the only plan for urban renewal in Uptown which has arisen spontaneously from the needs and participation of neighborhood residents, and as such is the plan which can best guarantee continuing participation of residents in the planning and retention of their community.

The UCCC wanted to avoid making a decision on the Hank Williams Village, and stated that the proposal would have to secure funding sources before any action can be taken. Within two months, council members were surprised to learn that the coalition had secured $475,000 in funds from individuals and businesses for construction. Salk, Ward & Salk, a major mortgage house, described the coalition proposal as economically feasible and agreed to pledge funds if the Federal Housing Administration would guarantee the loan. Harvey Rawson, Chairman of the Reality Company of America, proposed his company for residential construction. The Ravenswood-Uptown Interfaith Fellowship (which was made up of 15 churches), the Young Patriots, and 9 of the 46 property owners within the proposed college area also pledged their support. For those land owners who did not want to participate in the program, funds would be raised to buy — or to help remodel and upgrade — their buildings under contracts that would ensure fairness.

Further, due to deceptive practices of the UCCC, Rodney Wright proposed that no decisions be made until a committee of poor community residents and UCCC representation be set up to make decisions on the plan. The discussion was tabled until the next monthly meeting. After the meeting, UCCC Chair Uranna Demofle further frustrated coalition members by her statement to a Chicago Tribune newspaper reporter: "Mr. Wright's discussion of commitments (UCCC) had been too vague. She said she did not know how much time will be required by the UCCC to study the situation and determine whether there is hope for a residential development for the proposed college site." The Patriots and the Poor People's Campaign felt that the village proposal had been presented in a clear and precise presentation, but once again community concerns were being ignored.

The UCCC had no intention of handing over a community victory, and as always performed their role as a rubber stamp for the Daley Machine. Then in a surprise UCCC meeting, where plans for a community/UCCC meeting were to be discussed, the village plans were referred to the Chicago City Council, which voted to approve the building of the Chicago City College. Daley had won again.

The Patriots knew that the UCCC and the Uptown Chicago Commission had to be dealt with in a more militant manner, and pledged to disrupt all remaining public meetings. We started charging the committee members with class hatred and prejudice against the poor, took over their meetings, disrupted their plans (and halted temporarily) their plans for a city college. Several committee members refused to come to public meetings, because they were afraid of the community residents and the militancy of the Young Patriots.

Higher Education

n the summer of 1969, plans were being made to locate a center from Chicago Teachers North into the Uptown community later becoming Northeastern Illinois University. Dr. Stanley Newman, who taught anthropology at the teachers' college, proposed the project, and the college was willing to fund it with federal and state support and scholarships from the Illinois Scholarship Commission.

Newman had grown up on the streets of New York. As a youth, he was a street gang member and could relate to the Uptown youth. Through the encouragement and support of community workers Newman changed his life and pursued a career in education while never forgetting his roots and those who helped him. He wanted to give back, so he chose Uptown, because he had heard of the people's struggles and the Young Patriots. His belief was that everyone should have a means to an education. As his co-director, he chose Dee Dee Mayberry, a well-known and dedicated social worker in Uptown and a socialist democrat.

Because I was studying for my GED and working with Uptown youth, I was asked to assist in developing outreach programs and a curriculum, and to co-teach a course on Appalachian history and migration, as a representative of the Young Patriots. The Uptown People's Northeastern University Center opened in June of 1969 as part of the college.

The purpose of center was to foster understanding of all racial, ethnic, and minority groups. A strong consensus was that the people of Uptown, as well as two other communities — South Lakeview and Lincoln Park — needed programs to develop the leadership potential of indigenous persons who were committed to using their skills to better communicate or to improve living conditions in their community or native lands. These skills could be accomplished by funding for education that had been denied to the poor. NEIU would offer tangible resources to help community residents design programs to alleviate poverty, pursue self-determination, and offer a more positive future — not to mention gain a college education.

The goals and courses of the center were created with the input of community groups and students. Drawing from the experiences of JOIN, the Young Patriots, the

People's School, and the history of people's struggles to organize, we were able to develop a curriculum centered around identified cultural, racial, and economic and class struggles. Courses included Organizing in Oppressed Communities, Community Organizing I and II, Community Resources, Community Dynamics I and II, Analysis of a Multi-Ethnic Community, History of Appalachian Culture and Migration, History and Culture of the Native American, History and Culture of Hispanic Americans and Migration, History and Culture of Japanese Americans, American Black History, and Community History of the Uptown, Lakeview and Lincoln Park Communities.

For students to receive five credits per course, they would have to complete fieldwork with assignments to outside groups of their choice, but not with groups that represented their culture and nationality, in order to get a better understanding of other people's customs and life-styles. Many organizations, such as the American Indian Center, Native American Committee, Japanese Service Committee, Latino Institute, Hull House Association, welcomed the students' participation.

Community students from Uptown traveled to the main campus, while many students from NEIU campus traveled to Uptown to attend classes there. The center was instrumental in the development of the Human Services Department at the main campus. I received a BA in Anthropology in 1973. Many more followed, and received degrees that would have been previously denied to them due to financial needs. After graduating, many students continued organizing in their respective communities or native lands.

Young Patriot Free Clinic

F or all of our talk about militancy, one of the things I am most proud of about our work was our Free Health Clinics. In September of 1969, the doors of the Young Patriots Free Health Clinic, located in an apartment at 1140 Sunnyside Avenue, was opened to the Uptown people. The clinic was totally administered by poor white migrants, mostly Southerners, and led by Bobby Joe McGinnis. The Panthers shared with us their contacts in the medical field, so our clinic had medical doctors and students from some of the most prestigious medical schools and hospitals in the country.

The recruitment of medical personnel was conducted by the Medical Core of Northwestern University Medical Union for Professional Services (MCPS), an affiliate of the Medical Committee for Human Rights, which was founded in 1964 in Mississippi to provide free health services to local residents. The recruits came from Northwestern University Medical School, University of Illinois Medical School, Presbyterian St. Luke's Hospital, and Billings Hospital, in addition to a well-known psychiatrist, Aaron Hilkovich. At its peak, the clinic boasted a staff of 10 volunteer doctors, 10 nurses, and 50 community volunteers. The medical volunteer staff covered all expenses.

Our clinic opened after regular working and school hours to accommodate the community, and particularly school-age children. Several services were offered, including tests for whooping cough, tuberculosis, pregnancy, lead poisoning, anemia, and syphilis. It also provided shots for polio and tetanus as well as physicals for those needing one for a job. Medical doctors would provide pro bono services for life threatening conditions and surgeries. Patients were never billed from the hospital. Qualified doctors would write prescriptions, with free samples provided as much as possible. When a patient had to go to a specialist, doctor or hospital, one of the volunteer doctors or a member of the Patient Advocacy Team, a special program set up to protect patient rights, would accompany them to ensure proper and fast service by medical and social service personnel.

According to a report by the Chicago Board of Health, Uptown had the highest infant mortality in Chicago and the nation as a whole, due to lead poisoning, malnutrition and the poor health of many children. Six hospitals operated in the Uptown area, in addition to one Board of Health Clinic, and the Young Patriots Free Clinic. Many residents were reluctant to go to hospitals that had formerly denied them services or treated them with disrespect.

Accessing healthcare services took a considerable amount of precious travel time that many could not afford. We organized a program of volunteers and professionals to transport patients or fund their transportation needs on public transportation. Uptown residents were also skeptical of the local hospitals because every time they visited the emergency room and the injury was determined to be suspicious, the hospital personnel would report it to the Chicago Police.

I was placed under suspicion when I had two broken fingers and visited the emergency room at Ravenswood Hospital. When I could offer no proof of insurance or cash payment, my hand was simply wrapped in surgical tape, and I was sent out of the emergency room without x-rays, examination or medication. The hospitals personnel reported me to the Chicago Police, who visited me the next day inquiring if I had gotten the injury from being involved in a fight. Weeks later, I received the emergency room bill.

The clinic was a huge success. In addition to healthcare, the clinic offered other community services such as the food pantry (which served over 350 families with a free breakfast for children program), free daycare for working mothers, and free legal services. We treated over 600 patients every month. But the City of Chicago and the Chicago Board of Health did not like the free clinics success, because they had no control over its operations. Many times, patients leaving the Young Patriots Clinic would be harassed, and sometimes have their medicine confiscated by the Chicago cops. The Red Squad constantly photographed both patients and the clinic staff. Many of the Young Patriots would pose for their photographs with "Power to the People" fists in the air. Sometimes on cold days, we would take the cops a warm cup of coffee to let them know that we knew they were watching us.

November of 1969 was the beginning of continuous surveillance and harassment by the FBI and the Chicago Police. Both agencies had contacted several members of the medical staff that were supporting the clinic. An article in the Chicago Tribune, dated December 31, 1969, reveals that Dr. Bruce Douglas, chairman of the Dental and Oral Surgery Department at Presbyterian-St. Luke Hospital and a candidate for the Illinois House of Representatives, was visited by two policemen from the Chicago Gang Intelligence Unit. They suggested to Dr. Douglas "that it might be wise for him to disavow any association with the Young Patriots." The doctor simply ignored their threats and continued supporting the clinic.

In December 1969, the Gang Intelligence Unit also

visited Alphonse Spanitz, the absentee landlord of the apartment building that housed the clinic. In an article in the Chicago Tribune, dated January 5, 1970, Spanitz stated that "around the middle of November I found out about the Young Patriots, and I told them that I had no objections as long the tenants in the 17-unit flat apartment building were not disturbed." In December, the landlord reported that he received complaints of a noisy Saturday-night party at the clinic, and he "kicked them out." McGinnis stated that "the clinic had been operating on Saturdays at that location for two months and had never had a party in the apartment." McGinnis also stated: "Anyone who lives in the neighborhood knows we don't have time for parties, and everyone knows that's not the reason we were kicked out."

According to Patriots attorney Ted Stein, "the Young Patriots charged that the clinic was ordered out of its home within hours after the police visit to Spanitz." Robert Brinkman, who was a medical student volunteer for the entire history of the clinic, stated that "during a clinic personnel meeting at the Sunnyside clinic location, cops made an attempt to raid the clinic because of a complaint of a loud party taking place, but were surprised to find personnel dressed in white medical smocks and could not show proof of the complaint."

The clinic was reopened the following week at 4408 Sheridan Road, which would eventually become the Young

Patriot Headquarters. Later, the clinic relocated across the street and took up an entire flat of offices. According to Jake Seigel, the owner of the building housing the clinic, he too was visited by the cops and was asked to evict the clinic. Seigel denied their request, because he supported what it was doing. Due to financial constraints, the Patriots relocated to Grace Street, where the clinic was evicted once again in 1972. I spoke with Seigel as early as September 2017, and he is still being harassed by the authorities, because he allows the homeless to occupy the space that was formally the Young Patriots Clinic.

The City of Chicago, the United States Board of Health, and the Chicago Board of Health did not like the success of the Young Patriots Clinic. The Chicago Board of Health challenged the clinic by opening a temporary clinic several blocks away in another part of Uptown. The city's clinic was federally funded by the War on Poverty program, under the Model Cities Program. The clinic was located one block from Lake Michigan on Clarendon Dr. in a wealthy part of Uptown. It operated Monday through Friday, from 8am to 5pm, and could only treat 25 clients a day. Most of those who were treated at the city's clinic would not return, because several poor residents said that they were mistreated by the doctor and staff — some were even told to "go home and bathe."

As expected, the Daley Machine filed for an ordnance that would require all clinics and drug abuse programs to provide the names of their patients to the Chicago Board of Health. The law would regulate only community-run and independent organizations, leaving private clinics exempt, although it included the Salvation Army's drug treatment program.

According to the Firing Line newspaper: "In Uptown, the powers this law potentially gives the Daley Machine would be enormous. The Young Patriots Community Health Services, the Emerald City Drug Abuse Center, the ADAPT program at the American Indian Center, and many other organizations would apparently not be able to operate without a license from the Chicago Board of Health."

Even if the law did pass, the Young Patriots vowed to keep the Community Clinic open, and refuse to give information to the Chicago Board of Health. The Black Panthers and the Young Lords were mobilizing people to protest the city's actions, and to "take to the streets, if necessary" — a statement that city officials were sure to understand. All three Rainbow Coalition organizations were fighting the same ordinance.

The Board of Health opposed all efforts to keep the clinic open. We demanded to know where the Chicago Board of Health was allocating its money. They were spending $3 per patient, while New York was spending $110.00 per patient. In 1966, voters had approved the issuing of several million dollars in bonds to construct community health clinics.

The court battle between the Board of Health and Young Patriots' lawyer Ted Stein would unexpectedly come to a temporary end a year later in July of 1970, when Associate Judge Nathan Kaplan ruled that the Young Patriots Clinic could continue to operate without a license, claiming that the ordinance was so vague that it was unenforceable. The people had won the battle, at least this time. Chicago would continue to challenge the Young Patriots in court.

Meanwhile, since the poor of Uptown could not get representation as in the governance of the local Model Cities, they set their sights on convincing the Board of Health Clinic to increase their hours of operation. The additional time would be spent on political education for residents to take ownership of their living conditions and strive for self-determination of their community, in order to stop oppression by the Daley Machine. A plan of action was devised to confront the Chicago Board of Health. Operation Red Ball was launched by the health services program and the Young Patriots to expose the lies of the Board of Health, involve people in struggles, and to demand immediate attention from the City of Chicago to the community's healthcare needs.

The Young Patriots never viewed their health services, or any of their programs, as being an alternative or a counter-institution. They saw them as a way of politically educating the people and getting them actively involved to change their community. People were not just objects to be used to run their programs, but were encouraged to take over and own their programs. The health services program was organized to effectively complete the main purpose of the Young Patriots to politically educate the people in class struggles, and work themselves out of a job by turning the clinic over to the patients and healthcare staff.

In creating the healthcare program, the Young Patriots felt that they were beginning to involve people to deal with health conditions by allowing people to intellectually grow in a political ideology and to become medically self-reliant. The healthcare program became an independent entity. Every patient was a member, and helped to carry out political programs in Uptown.

We challenged the Chicago Board of Health Clinic in Uptown by organizing as many people as possible to flood the clinic with patients, and to demand the clinic add additional weekday and weekend hours. On Friday November 6, 1970, members of the Young Patriots and Uptown Area Peoples Planning Coalition, along with representatives from several Native American tribes, Blacks, and Latinos conducted a sit-in at the Chicago Board of Health clinic located at 4141 N. Clarendon in Uptown. About 80 protesters occupied the building, and the Patriots brought four doctors, three nurses, and three social workers with them. The Young Patriots doctors offered their assistance, but it was declined because the doctors had not gone through the Board of Health's administrative procedures.

Although all measures were taken to keep operation Red Ball a secret, information was leaked, and both the FBI and the City of Chicago police were there to meet the protesters. Everyone`s name was gathered and stored in the FBI files. At 4:30pm, the protesters were warned that anyone still in the clinic at 5pm would be arrested. Children were taken home, and at 5pm the police and FBI arrested 23 women and 20 men, and charged them with trespassing. All the Young Patriots doctors were arrested. A rally was organized the next day, where the Board of Health clinic was discredited in the community. As a result of the sit-in and rally, Operation Red Ball did force the clinic to expand its hours, as well as add additional staff. Later, all charges were dropped because of pressure exerted by the community and the medical staff, who charged that the city clinic had discriminated against the poor.

Each patient that came to the Young Patriots Clinic for services was administered a urine test to identify possible health problems. Due to the high percentage of patients with kidney related health problems, the Health Services Committee instituted Operation Yellow Ball. A physician volunteer at the Young Patriots Clinic managed to secure a federal grant to conduct research and treatment in kidney disorders caused by lead poisoning. He presented a proposal to the Young Patriots and the Health Services Committee to sponsor the research. It would be a monumental task that would require three thousand samples. Our only stipulation was that any patient identified as needing services would be given free treatment. The operation was a huge endeavor that required the participation of schools, churches, parent groups and daycare centers, not to mention door-to-door volunteers. Over four thousand samples were collected. History was made, because a screening of this size has never been conducted in a community.

These campaigns proved that medical care can be taken to the community, and residents can be involved in their medical needs. We established that people can plan for their medical needs without the control of city, state or federal governments. It was also very helpful in letting the community know that the Young Patriots were there to serve them. Many lives were saved, and many life-threatening illnesses were avoided from the research.

Chicago is Burning

We also had to confront the epidemic of arson. In 1973, Peggy Terry was interviewed by Studs Terkel for his book *P.S. Tales From a Lifetime of Listening*, in which she describes arson in Uptown and its tragic consequences:

They're burning the place down at night. Winos come to us because we've helped them. They come to us and tell us who paid them to set fire to certain buildings. We run one of the free health clinics in Chicago, the Young Patriots Clinic. They come to us and tell us that they set fire to buildings. They burned one of our children to death. They burned one of our children, who came to the clinic on Saturday. Saturdays are set aside for children, and they burned one of our children to death. How can you fight this? You wake up in the middle of the night and your building is on fire, and all you can do is flee. You live in absolute terror. Not only from the police, but fire, of your children strung out on dope. A ghetto is a ghetto, and color has nothing to do with it.

Night fire patrols were organized by the Intercommunal Survival and the Heart of Uptown Coalitions to catch arsonists in the act of committing crimes. Helen Schiller, Chicago City Council Alderwoman for Uptown, stated that "two Chicago firemen were caught and arrested for setting fire to garages in the community."

According to Bob Rehak's *Uptown: A portrait of a Chicago Neighborhood in the Mid-1970s*, arson in Chicago increased 182% between 1974 and 1977. This increase was so alarming that the state adopted a resolution on December 12, 1976, directing the Illinois Legislature Investigating Commission to explore causes and make recommendations. Years later, the Heart of Uptown Coalition and the "20/20" television news program investigated the fires and proved the burned buildings were the result of arson, and 16 people were burned to death. No one has been brought to justice to pay any compensation to the victims' families, or incarcerated for the murders.

Fighting For Solidarity and Racial Equality

The issues that the Civil Rights Movement was focusing on in Black communities were similar to those that we had identified in Uptown and other poor white communities in the United States. The Young Patriots were about building strong alliances with all poor peoples by exposing the conditions of the poor whites compared to those of other racial and minority poor communities.

We hated racism and white supremacy. Racism was a demon that had to be driven out and slain if we were going to have unity with other groups. This was consistent with our belief that all people have a right to self-determination and freedom. For many, fighting the demons of racism may not seem monumental, but for many of us raised in an environment of indifference to other groups and fed a steady diet of racism and segregation, it was a gigantic demon to be slain. We had to change to make life tolerable, and have some sort of meaning. We were used to change. On a daily basis, our entire life was about changing, and living in Uptown influenced us to change to meet adversity head on. We came to realize that if we were experiencing the conditions of adversity, then other groups, like people of color and others, were experiencing them too.

In the days of JOIN, two black women — Big Dovie Thurman and her daughter Little Dovie Coleman — joined the group and founded the Welfare Recipients Demand Action, a group that fought for the rights of welfare recipients. The Harpers, a racially mixed married couple, also became involved in housing issues, and were very accepted by the community. A Black Cuban refugee also began to hang out with us and became a member of the Young Patriots.

Solidarity isn't just a word. It is a process, and sometimes it is an uncomfortable process. Not only was racism a central issue in our efforts to liberate our people, we also began to develop a new awareness of the gay, lesbian and women's liberation movements that were gaining popularity and demanding liberation in the US and around the world. Like most people, we were raised to believe that the only union must be between a man and a woman. Southern evangelists preached that homosexuals were a creation of the devil, and that the Holy Bible taught that a woman is unequal to a man, and therefore his helper.

Gay men were not respected in Uptown, and especially with street people. If a person exhibited homosexual behavior, he would be treated as an outcast. Some guys were involved in what was called "queer baiting," a street term used as baiting a hook for fishing, which meant hustling queers. For some, it was a means of making money, and being a "hustler" was not always looked upon as being a "homosexual," because it was a means of survival. Some however would rob the homosexual and beat them.

Lesbians were not a threat to the street guys' masculinity. Some would fantasize about sexual acts between two women. Very few considered women to be equal to men, and would use violence against women when they disobeyed them. Convincing many in Uptown that gay people and women were their equals was a difficult task, but we knew that we had to defend the rights of all oppressed people. We wanted equality for everyone. It would be counterrevolutionary if we did not view homosexuals as first a human being, and both women and homosexuals as equal to men. The terms "faggot" and "punk" are to be deleted from our vocabulary, in addition to "the little woman," that many would use to identify our sisters.

Because of peer and street group pressure, it was difficult to change all that we wanted to change. But there was minimal success, and over a period of time, as the gay and women's liberation movement grew and gained more popularity, some street guys did start to change their behavior. But the members of Patriots did change, and continued to educate our people on equality and respect for all people.

Although Uptown was a melting pot, representing practically every nationality and race in the world, there were very few Black people living in the community. A small pocket lived in the in the north end of Uptown. We had very little contacts with them, due to Uptown being primarily a Southern white community. Still, those who were there were cautious when they would be on the streets, or going to and from work. A few Blacks would travel from other parts of the city to work in fast food restaurants and as domestic workers for those living in the more affluent Lakefront that bordered Uptown's to the east. They were rarely seen and were not involved in community programs. They were only there for their jobs.

Some Blacks came from "Sundowner" towns in the South, and were very cautious not to be seen at night. The term "Sundowner," as explained by a Black Alabama resident meant: "Don't let your Black ass get caught after sundown in this town." I very seldomly saw Black people in Uptown after sundown until 1969, when more were driven out of their communities by urban renewal and forced to settle in Uptown.

We believed that the Appalachian states were, much

like Puerto Rico, treated like a colony of the United States. The US government had neglected sharing its wealth and resources with people who were only recognized as resources to be exploited by the coal and textile industry, military recruitment, and a forgotten people by politicians. Since there was not much taxable wealth due to low wages, major resources to help the people out of poverty was given to other wealthier states. People were left to scratch out a living by any means possible and were reduced to low level servitude.

This was the message that the Young Patriots would use as an organizing tool. We would explain how these conditions in Chicago and nationally kept poor Southern whites in poverty by being denied proper healthcare, job training, and employment assistance. They were stereotyped as being backwards and treated by the majority population as a separate entity of the United States, as was brought to light by Michel Harrington's book, *The Other America*.

The Patriots was a predominantly young Southern white male organization. Other groups were represented — Puerto Rican Angelo Sanchez and Cuban Roberto Alarcon were members — and women were welcomed into the organization. Peggy Terry was considered a member. Carol Blakely (Doug Youngblood's wife), Mary Ellen Keniston, Kit Komatsu (an original Freedom Rider), Marcella Geary (Uptown Area People's Planning Coalition

Chairman Chuck Geary's daughter) were all charter members and had equal decision-making power as the male members.

We began by sending out a friendly statement introducing ourselves to Uptown residents, emphasizing social change. The statement called for fair treatment by the police, adequate housing, and recreational areas for kids, and for schools to meet the needs of the children. It also informed the community that we would be opening a storefront office, and that everyone is welcome to offer suggestions, because uptown is our home and we need to control our neighborhood. As a follow up to the statement, members of the Young Patriots went door to door to talk about neighborhood problems.

The statement received positive responses and suggestions from residents. Some started coming to meetings while others would give us encouragement and donations. On occasion, winos would offer us a drink of their port wine. Out of respect, we accepted their gift and encouragement. These were the beginning stages of the Young Patriots organizing in the community.

As Uptown resident, John Dawson, told Hollander and Gitlin, "Until people in this country come to think and realize that they can run, rule this country, it's gonna be in a hell of a shape. If the people here in this neighborhood had of woke up to what is goin' on ten years ago, this neighborhood wouldn't be like it is today."

To say that we were only looking out for others is a false representation of who we were. We wanted freedom, equality and respect as much as we wanted to help others get theirs. We wanted justice for the wrongs that had been done to the people in our community. Most importantly, we wanted the residents of Uptown to know what we had learned, and asked them to join us in attempting to alleviate the pain caused by broken homes, unjust incarcerations, unequal economic and social systems, poverty and disrespect. We tried to convince them that their marginalization was not their fault, but rather due to a capitalist system that favored corporate profits over human lives. Collectively, we argued, they could make a difference in their own lives.

Convincing them would be a great achievement, because Southerners are very difficult to organize. They will very seldom come to meetings, and were very suspicious of anyone invading their privacy. We told them that we cared and asked them for specific examples of how changes could be made. Protest marches were another concern for older family members. The Patriots explained that they were not about marching, but rather resistance to authorities that controlled their lives. The biggest hurdle for us to overcome was their faith.

Culturally Southern people are fundamentalist Christians, believing that God put government officials in power and guided their decisions. We had to convince them that their faith allows them to protest and question their elected officials' decisions when they don't fit with God's word. That the Uptown churches wanted them out of their community. And that God would not want them to be treated like the way they are being treated in Chicago.

Due to the nature of the neighborhood, there were few churches in Uptown, most of which did not serve the poor population. The St. Thomas of Canterbury Catholic Church, Edgewater Baptist Church, Ebenezer Lutheran Church, and the First Evangelical Free Church all professed to helping the poor, but none had a program to serve the poor outside of their missionary ministries. Most of the Southerners were Baptist, but felt uncomfortable and unwelcome, due to not possessing "proper church clothing," or money to donate. They were treated as lower class and outsiders while attending the Edgewater Baptist Church, which was located in a community north of Uptown and attended mostly by middle-class residents along the Lakefront. Many in this community supported the "revitalization" of Uptown. St Thomas of Canterbury Catholic Church also supported the urban renewal of Uptown.

Occasionally, outside individuals would come into the community and pretend to be preachers, collecting the meager tithes that the poor possessed. But eventually, the unscrupulous individual would be found a fraud and asked to leave the community, sometime violently. Many Southern families held church services in their apartments, with the most knowledgeable Christian family member leading the service.

This was the beginning of our outreach. From that time on, we began organizing and lending support to grassroots groups and organizations. Conversations with people on the street convinced them to come out to community meetings and protests. As our support grew, we noticed more police surveillance, and several members began to receive threats of physical harm that we were sure was coming from the cops.

The idea of a revolution was different for us than it was for the college students. The language used by students and other activists was not familiar to us. They would use technical terms like petite bourgeoisie, proletariat, indigenous, oligarchy, misogynist and others. It is not that we could not educate ourselves, we did. Oftentimes, after a conversation, we would scratch our head and ask, "What the fuck did they say?" We had to do it our own way. Any organizing had to directly come from our own understanding of the situation, and not from outside political activists. Our revolution had to start locally with the residents of Uptown. As most of us did not know much about the national movement, we wanted the revolution to be community-based.

To further their training, members of the Patriots conducted and participated in workshops about Southern migration and resistance at the Highlander Folk School in

Tennessee, currently known as the Highlander Research and Education Center. Highlander was established in 1932 as a social justice training school and cultural center, and provided training and educational workshops for union and labor activists who were fighting for better conditions for coal miners. In the 1950's, Highlander changed its focus and organized workshops and training sessions in nonviolent protest strategies for the Civil Rights Movement. Dr. Martin Luther King, Rosa Parks, John Lewis and Eleanor Roosevelt attended workshops on civil rights at Highlander.

It was important to teach our people that the middle and upper classes enjoyed their wealth due to the poor and working class laboring at minimum or low wages. Many middle-class liberals wanted to help the poor, but knew they could never live the life of the poor. Later, we would rely on many churches, fraternities, and social groups to support our programs.

We understood that many of the people that we wanted to communicate our ideas to were not politically illiterate, but had their own view of the political process. Politics and politicians have always victimized them. We did not want to be viewed as politicians who made promises and could not be trusted. Our approach had to be very careful not to alienate them with too much political or militant rhetoric as many in the student movement were doing.

Our philosophy was that we could organize poor

white and working-class people, because we were poor, white and working class. But we still needed to maintain our identity as street people. It took about a year for residents to identify the Patriots as a credible organization alongside the Peacemaker street gang. Young street people agreed with us changing and serving the community. Many community residents were confused, as some of the Peacemaker gang were still in the community and continuing their gang activities.

The cops, local politicians, and establishment organizations, such as the Council of the Southern Mountains Chicago Southern Center and the Chicago Boys Club identified us as a gang. The Chicago Southern Center refused our association. We believed that was because they received major funding from insurance magnet W. Clement Stone of the Combined Insurance Company, a Mayor Richard Daley supporter even though he was a Republican.

We were fighting against the gang image, but we knew why gangs were doing what they do. We remained friends with gang members who accepted us, and sometime they would visit us and listen to our programs and agree not to interfere with our work. Many times, the commonality of living conditions made it much easier to organize and get residents to attend meetings.

Shoot to Kill

The assassination of Martin Luther King brought great anxiety to Patriots — not only was he murdered by a white man, but it took place in the South. Many Southerners were afraid that there might be retaliation from people of color, and they did not know what to expect. When necessary, Young Patriots would go into the streets and bars, talk to the residents, and let them know that if any trouble did arise, we were ready to de-escalate. Many Young Patriots joined the Young Lords at the Church of the Three Crosses, in case the heat did begin to come back to the neighborhoods.

No problems occurred, mainly because most of the Uptown cops were temporally assigned to other communities of unrest. What did concern us came several days later when riots broke out in several Black communities, and Mayor Daley issued his famous "shoot to kill" order. Residents of Uptown felt that they also would be targeted by the cops. At a City Hall Press Conference, Daley ordered his police to "To shoot to kill any arsonist, to shoot to maim or cripple," anyone looting any store in Chicago. We knew the order made it legal for the cops to continue doing what they had always been doing in Uptown and other poor communities in Chicago. And we knew that there would be unnecessary deaths. We were right in those assumptions.

On Monday, April 15, the *Sun Times* newspaper in Chicago headline read: "Story Behind Riot Toll: The Nine Who Died." The newspaper identified the nine who died as statistics in the midst of "general turmoil." To avoid offending Daley, the newspaper did not truthfully report what the two reporters had written about the nine killed in the riots. After much protest by Joel Havemann and Ben W. Heineman, the original writers of the article, the *Sun Times* retracted the story and stated that the biggest mystery involved the deaths of four men shot in one small area of W. Madison Street in a three-and-a-half-hour span. The article explains: "One victim was shot in the back when he and his wife entered an alley to avoid police. The man was protecting his wife by covering her with his body when he was shot. Two other men were shot inside stores. A fourth was a 24-year-old man shot in an alley. His sister said he was just a bystander."

On April 17, after international and local criticism Daley held a press conference denying his order to kill, saying: "There wasn't any shoot to kill order. They say that I gave orders to shoot down children. I said to the super-intendent, if a man has a Molotov cocktail in his hand and throws it into a building with children and women above, he should be shot right there, and if I were there, I would shoot him. Everybody knows it was twisted around, and they say Daley gave orders to shoot children. That wasn't true." What was even more bizarre was when a reporter asked Daley's press secretary about the mayor's denial of his "shoot to kill" order. The secretary simply blamed it on the reporters, saying "they should have printed what he meant and not what he said."

Havemann later said, "There's little doubt there was a rogue police unit targeting people on that Friday." We knew about rogue police units. We were safe during the unrest, because they were busy targeting our Black broth-ers and sisters. He wasn't sure, however, if the rogue unit committed the murders.

If Daley couldn't control Chicago after Dr. King's assassination, he was determined to do so during the Democratic National Convention a few months later in August, 1968. He was going to prove to the world that no one comes to his city and causes disorder. After threats that thousands of demonstrators were going to take over Lincoln Park on the city's lakefront and spike the water supply with LSD, Daley was able to assemble one of the largest security forces in the history of Chicago. In addition to his gang of 12,000 Chicago policemen, he asked the governor of Illinois to mobilize 5,000 National Guardsmen, 6,000 specially trained army troops, several hundred state and county lawmen, and a large number of secret service and private security service workers. The security totaled well over 25,000, while the anti-Vietnam War protesters who arrived for the convention numbered only a few thousand. The City of Chicago had become an armed camp.

When the convention began, it was Daley's and the Chicago police gang's time to take revenge. He had not forgotten how the press exposed his "shoot to kill" order. The Chicago Police also had taken an ass kicking from the press, and were still pissed that eight of their own were jailed after the Summerdale police scandal. They were ready to bust some heads and to show everyone that Daley was the boss. The police were Chicago's largest gang, and Daley was their leader. The mayor was convinced that by unleashing overwhelming force, the protests would remain under control.

The situation escalated when sharp disagreements about the Vietnam War broke out between the delegates on the convention floor. A faction led by Eugene McCarthy demanded an end to the war. This position was challenged by presidential candidate Hubert Humphrey, who supported the war. Fights broke out, and several delegates were beaten by the police.

Outside the convention, police and National Guard began to indiscriminately gas, beat and arrest protesters, reporters, clergy, and anyone that got in their way. On the convention floor, a delegate pleaded with Daley to stop the senseless brutality happening outside. From footage that contains no sound, Daley seems to be saying to the delegate, "Fuck you, motherfucker!" The battle was caught on television and broadcast all over the world, showing that Chicago — a city in a country built on democracy — was actually a police state run by a dictator who would go to any extreme to control his empire.

Just a few months before the Democratic National Convention, the Anti-Riot Act (also known as the "H. Rap Brown Law," after the former Minister of Justice with the Black Panther Party) was passed as a response to the urban riots of 1964-1967. The law was intended to deter outside instigators who did not live in local communities. It targeted anyone who "uses interstate or foreign commerce or uses any facility of interstate commerce, including but not limited to, the mail, telegraph, telephone, radio, on television, with intent A) to incite a riot, B) to organize, promote, encourage, participate in, or carry on a riot, or C) to commit any act of violence in furtherance of a riot act; or D) to aid or abet any person in inciting or participating in or carrying on a riot or community any act of violence in furtherance of a riot."

Eight activists, who became known as the Chicago 8, were arrested and charged with inciting riots during the Democratic Convention. They were Abbie Hoffman and Jerry Rubin (founders and leaders of the Yippies), Tom Hayden (founder of Students for a Democratic Society), Dave Dillinger (pacifist and conscientious objector), Bobby Seale (Black Panther Party founder), in addition to John Froines, Lee Weiner and Rennie Davis (Moratorium to End the War in Vietnam and JOIN organizer). All but Froines and Weiner were found guilty of violating the Anti-Riot Act. Because of his outburst in court and being Black, Bobby Seal was sentenced to four years in prison. The convictions were later overturned on appeal.

Due to the widespread media coverage of the violence at the Chicago Democratic Convention, the Walker Commission was appointed by the federal government to investigate the interaction of the protesters with the Chicago Police. The commission published its findings in the Walker Report, concluding that what happened amounted to a "police riot" directed at protesters. The Chicago Police Department was the only police force in the United States that was accused of a police riot by the Presidents Commission on Violence, directed by Daniel Walker, a businessman and a staff of over thirty. The report states:

The nature of the response was unrestrained and indiscriminate police violence on many occasions, particularly at night. The violence was made all the more shocking by the fact that it was often inflicted upon persons who had broken no law, disobeyed no order, made no threat. These included peaceful demonstrators, onlookers, and a large number of residents who were simply passing through, or happened to live in, the areas where confrontations were occurring.

Most of us stayed away from the protests. Our protests were local and stayed in Uptown, just as Blacks and Hispanics remained in their neighborhoods. Protesters had our sympathies and support, but our involvement would have only brought more attention to Uptown, especially if any one of us was arrested. Members of the Young Patriots knew that they would surely be charged with bogus crimes and imprisoned due to our activities in Uptown. The Young Lords in Lincoln Park believed the same would happen to them if they attended the protest. Instead, they offered medical care to injured protesters, while we offered refuge.

We knew the Chicago Police, and strongly believed that Daley would never relinquish power to anyone. The cops beat anyone and everyone who stood in their way. It made no difference if they were reporters, clergy, women, teenagers or innocent bystanders, Daley and his gang were going to do to them what they had been doing to the poor of Chicago for decades. During the Democratic Convention, he was challenged by delegates and elected officials to stop the beatings, but their requests fell on deaf ears, as many were injured and jailed. Because members of the press were beaten indiscriminately, they finally believed that what the poor had been saying about being victims of the city government and the Chicago Police was true. Daley, for his part, never admitted any wrongdoing.

The Rainbow Coalition

Rainbow Coalition: "A group (such as a political coalition) whose members are of different ethnic, political, or religious background." — MERRIAM WEBSTER DICTIONARY

The Young Patriots' activities were being monitored by the Black Panther Party led by Deputy Chairman Fred Hampton and Cha-Cha Jimenez of the Young Lords Organization. Jimenez, a former gang member, had come to embrace revolutionary politics while in prison. Hampton came to believe that the revolution could not be won without the poor and working class of all colors.

Jimenez was already identifying with Southern whites that were members of a North Side gang located on Sheffield Avenue. They called themselves the Rebels, and one of their leaders was Puerto Rican. The Black Panthers knew the Young Patriots by working with us in the Cleaver-Terry presidential campaign. We were approached by Bobby Lee, Field Secretary for the Illinois Chapter of the Black Panthers, and someone the YPO had met at a Lincoln Park Citizens meeting, to become a part the Rainbow Coalition with the Young Lords Organization.

The Black Panther Party for Self Defense, founded in 1966 in Oakland, California by Huey P. Newton and Bobby Seale, was a Black political organization that provided a revolutionary model of serving the people with a Ten Point program that guided their activities. Initially, they started as an organization to combat police brutality through police monitoring patrols, which later grew into a broader effort to serve their community with Survival Programs Pending Revolution, free medical services, breakfast for children, and legal services, among others. The Panthers grew rapidly, establishing 38 chapters across the US. At the time, the Panthers were more militant than the Patriots, but we could identify with their service to the people. Their model was enormously influential on us. Bob Lee gave us a lot of great guidance on how to adapt their Survival Programs to our community.

The Young Lords Organization started in 1959 as a Puerto Rican street gang, doing what most street gangs do — fighting those who they believed to be their enemies, including whites, blacks and those of Hispanic origins, or whoever invaded their turf. In 1968, the gang changed from street fighting to a political organization. While in the Cook County Jail, the gang's leader Jimenez was influenced by radical prisoners. When he was released, he convinced the gang that gang banging was actually hurting the Lincoln Park neighborhood as well as dividing them from the people and organizations that were fighting for a better neighborhood.

Jimenez believed in revolution and uprising of protests by people both from Wicker Park and later when Puerto Ricans population were again being pushed out of Lincoln Park by Urban Renewal. While protesting imperialism in Puerto Rico was the solution to their freedom from oppression of the capitalist system that had held them down for too long. Their program was called "Educate to Liberate." The Lords' activities caught the attention of Fred Hampton, who was Chairman of the Illinois Chapter of the Black Panther Party, and he invited them to form a partnership with the Black Panthers, which would become known as the "Original Rainbow Coalition."

The Lords got more involved in addressing the needs of their community. They led demonstrations against police brutality, for women's rights, welfare rights, economic and social equality, as well as self-determination for their community and Puerto Rico. They adopted some of the Black Panther programs, such as the Emeterio Betances Health Clinic, free daycare centers, free dental clinics, a Puerto Rican Cultural Center, and a free breakfast for children program.

As with Uptown and other poor communities, urban

renewal was also targeting Lincoln Park, which was prime real estate, and desired by many developers. Mayor Daley established the Urban Renewal Conservation Council, consisting of all white, middle-class members. Again, like Uptown, this was a rubber stamp committee to carry out Daley's wishes.

Jimenez had learned a valuable lesson from the past. In 1958, the City of Chicago began the urban renewal program by expanding the downtown borders into Wicker Park, moving the poor and mostly Puerto Rican community into Lincoln Park, then a rundown neighborhood, and promising replacement housing for those who were displaced. The promise was not kept. Instead, the city replaced the community with Old Town and the Carl Sandburg Village, which were predominately white and middle class.

The Young Lords were not about to be pushed around by Mayor Daley. Jimenez and 250 protesters occupied an empty lot on Halsted Street and Armitage Avenue, which was designated for tennis courts. Instead, the people demanded the city build a park for children to have a place to play and families to enjoy.

Like us, the Young Lords posed the biggest threat to the cops. Because of their visibility in their community, they were major targets for Daley's police gang. Jimenez was arrested 18 times. The joke was that if we wanted to reach him, we should call the Cook County Jail first, because they always knew where to find him, or that we should start a gas fund for his lawyer, Jeffery Haas. Police beatings, harassment, false arrests and murder were a part of the plan. Even off-duty cops were in on the game: Manuel Ramos, a youth member of the Young Lords, was shot dead by an off-duty cop. The shooting lead to a massive march of 2,000 people on Daley's Bridgeport neighborhood. The Young Patriots, the Black Panthers and SDS were in attendance.

All murders are tragic, but the killing of Reverend Bruce Johnson and his wife Eugena was particularly brutal. Reverend Johnson was a pastor at the Armitage Methodist Church, and a strong supporter of the Young Lords. He wanted to provide them with a space to run a breakfast program and a daycare center. On Sunday, September 28, 1969, he and his wife were murdered. The reverend was warned to distance himself from the Young Lords. Today, no one has been held accountable in these murders. It still remains a cold case in the Chicago Police files.

Early 1968 was the beginning of planning the Rainbow Coalition in a meeting that included Jimenez, Lee, and representatives of the Students for a Democratic Society. The Young Patriots officially entered into the national radical movement in April 1968, and the official public announcement of the formation of the coalition was during a press conference in December 1968. This was a necessary move if we were going to be serious about making changes in Uptown. We wanted to show the nation that poor Southern whites would stand beside their Black and brown brothers and sisters in revolutionary solidarity to fight for freedom. It was time for us to walk the talk.

Why would the Black Panthers and Young Lords welcome whites, who have traditionally been their oppressors, into the coalition as equals? Many in the community had been active for several years organizing programs and action groups to build a better quality of life for Uptown residents. Fred Hampton knew of the Summerdale Police march and the Cleaver-Terry presidential campaign, and recognized that many of us were willing to fight for justice. We were welcomed into the coalition due to our anti-racist politics, and because we were a group that had proven that many members had evolved from street gang members and poor oppressed Southern whites into community organizers, much the same as many members of the Black Panthers and Young Lords had evolved. We adopted many of the Panther programs. They also recognized that we were targets for the cops and Mayor Daley, much the same as they were in their communities. The three organizations were an odd fit for a coalition, yet all three were fighting to break down racial and class barriers.

Alongside the Rainbow Coalition and inspired by it, Rising Up Angry began organizing in the Logan Square neighborhood in Chicago. They later joined the coalition, after adopting many of its survival programs, such as a free health clinic, breakfast program, free legal services, and a

GI program for returning Vietnam war veterans. Of major importance was Angry's powerful newspaper of the same name, which reached thousands of readers, informing them about their activities. Their philosophy was that of the Rainbow Coalition's — to unite poor communities to fight racism and the oppressiveness of the capitalist system.

Rising Up Angry was comprised of many SDS students who left JOIN after the community-student split, and used the JOIN model to organize working-class whites in Logan Square, another poor Chicago community. It was a perfect fit for Mike James, Diane Fager, Bob Lawson, Pat Sturgis, Nora Davis, Steve Tappis, James Cardea, and other students who had successfully organized with Southern street people. Some were called greasers. The greaser subculture was identified as individual gang members made up predominately of working and lower-working class whites, originally from the Southern and Eastern United States in the 1940's and 1950's. Photographs from the early days of Angry show that members of the Young Patriots attended their activities and social events.

We saw the benefits of being a part of the Rainbow Coalition as being extraordinary for us, because it was the beginning of a more powerful local union that the Daley Machine could not ignore. There was power in numbers, and that we could have support for our causes, especially after having gained support from all racial groups in Uptown. Further, it was a good move for the Patriots, because they were not seeking national attention, but it could not hurt our cause.

While filming in Chicago during the Democratic National Convention in 1968, filmmakers Mike Grey and Howard Alk of the Film Group heard about the relationship between the Panthers and "Hillbillies," who came together to organize the poor in their communities under the umbrella of the Rainbow Coalition. They knew that this coalition was an historical event. Never before had Southern whites and Blacks gotten together in Chicago to organize for identical revolutionary purposes. A portion of the film follows Bob Lee, a Black Panther organizer and the Young Patriots meeting with Uptown residents to announce the coalition between the Black Panthers and the Young Patriots. Racial tension did exist, and we were prepared to defend the Panthers presence in the community.

The success of the meeting was one of unity. Most residents attending had looked upon the Panthers with suspicion, but that changed after hearing that the same conditions of poverty, police brutality, slum living, class hatred existed in the Black and Hispanic communities. The meeting had broken down crucial racial barriers in Uptown. The film, American Revolution II, was released in April of 1969. It was banned from every major movie theater in Chicago by the Daley machine. Finally, Playboy Theatre owner Hugh Heffner would go against the wishes of Daley and allow the film to be previewed. The Three

Penny Cinema ran the film for thirty days.

We were met with suspicion by some of the members of the Black Panthers and Young Lords, due to the history of slavery and racism of the white Southern people. Both groups lost some members, but most welcomed us as their equal, because they saw the time had come for all peoples to put aside their differences and unite under the umbrella of the Rainbow Coalition. The leadership of both the Black Panthers and the Young Lords believed that the purge was necessary and beneficial to them, because both organizations had moved from using differences and conflict with other racial, ethnic and minority groups, to one of class struggle. The Young Patriots were identified by them as worthy of joining their coalition, because we had proven that even with our history of slavery and racism, we were fighting the same cause.

There was a strong understanding that self-determination must remain the main focus in forming the coalition. The coalition would stand for unity, but each member-group would operate independently within their own communities. Under this umbrella, the coalition would act as one group and support each other's causes. The understanding was if any basic changes were to come about in America for the poor and oppressed, and for changes to have longevity, they would have to come from the grassroots, because the poor knew how to solve their problems, if they were given the programs and resources.

If the poor and oppressed could solve their problems, then it would be a giant step in alleviating poverty and oppression in America, in addition to putting an end to the many government-sponsored agencies that imposed unreachable goals and guidelines on the poor, while using them as statistics for future funding.

We took inspiration from the Panthers in other ways. They wrote a Ten Point program outlining their demands and vision for a better society. We modeled ours after this, and wrote an Eleven Point program, which was intended to address eliminating class structures and allow workers to control wealth that comes from what they produce. Like the Panther's program, ours addressed immediate survival needs within the context of basic human rights. We asserted that food, clothing, shelter and medical care should be seen as basic human rights.

We embraced the idea, first put forward by the Panthers, that the people must control the police, and that the police must live in the community they patrolled. Today, it is common for activists to talk about a school-to-prison pipeline. In our platform, we pointed out that schools in poor communities are run like prisons and demanded that poor children be given the same education and materials as wealthy students. We identified racism as a tool of the capitalists, and called for an end to the draft and the American war in Vietnam. Perhaps the most important part of our program was: "To create revolutionary solidarity with all oppressed people and countries to create national liberation."

We had several approaches to education, by using printed materials (leaflets, books, and films), through discussion groups, and by example. As Doug Youngblood put it: "The Young Patriots understood from examining social movements in this country that militancy and programs designed to mitigate People's suffering without affecting the balance of power were inadequate and ineffective, and that if they were to avoid the mistakes of others, then their approach must show clearly from the start where they stood. With this in mind, they formulated, published and distributed copies of their 11-point program." Militancy was our only solution to our problems. Pacifism and compromise with the power structure had been a failure for the poor. Militancy had to be a tool to reach revolution, even if it meant violence.

It was commonly believed that the real reason that members of the Young Patriots and the Rainbow Coalition were under continual observation by the Chicago Police and the FBI was due to the first point of the Eleven Point program — the call to "eliminate class structures and to allow workers to control what they produce." The idea was that it was the poor and working class who could end the problems caused by capitalism, and that private property needed to be abolished. Not private property of homes, cars, clothing, etc., but the abolition of the private ownership of factories, utilities, communication and transportation systems, natural resources, and educational and medical services.

We found that the Young Patriots' support for other Rainbow members posed a real threat to the Daley machine and J. Edgar Hoover of the FBI. The presence of the Young Patriots in the coalition dispelled the illusion that Southern whites and Blacks could not unite. As a show of solidarity, we served as security for a Black Panther rally at Chicago's band shell in Grant Park and at the United Front Against Fascism in Oakland, California. In Chicago, Hampton addressed the crowd and praised us for our support, stressing the uniqueness of Southern whites working alongside Blacks.

This support and solidarity brought more police harassment and violence against the Young Patriots. Jakobi Williams, author of *From the Bullet to the Ballot: The Illinois Chapter of the Black Panther Party and Racial Coalition Politics in Chicago* explains, "Many of the police who patrolled Uptown were former members of white street gangs that used to clash with future members of the Young Patriots during their high school days. Scores of these officers were also Southern white migrants who sympathized with white supremacist groups and despised the Patriots for working with the Black Panthers." Many of the cops had ties to the underworld. I knew of a truck being hijacked and a load of whiskey stolen with the assistance of some

Chicago cops. As with other crimes being committed with police assistance, if I were to report the theft, I would surely be putting my life in danger. It was safer to just look the other way.

At the beginning of the Rainbow Coalition, we understood that there would be more surveillance of the Chicago Police. But we did not expect it to intensify as quickly as it did. The FBI COINTELPRO Unit alone was manned by more than 2,000 full-time FBI agents across the country. These agents were supported by more than 2,000 informers, each of whom was paid $300 a month.

COINTELPRO (Counterintelligence Program) was a program of the Federal Bureau of Investigation Agency that operated between 1956 and 1971. Its mission was to run covert operations to gather information on groups and individuals, and to eliminate radical and opposition groups within the United states that the FBI deemed to be subversive, or a threat to national security. FBI Director J. Edgar Hoover had a particular dislike for the Panthers. So, we found ourselves alongside the Black Panthers, being subjected to repression, blatant harassment and political prosecution of political crimes.

The COINTELPRO program used fraud, false news articles, letters and surveillance to categorize us as a sub-versive group along with other groups and individuals, such as Martin Luther King, NAACP, American Indian Movement, women's rights groups, SDS, and even Albert

Einstein. As Ward Churchill in the *The COINTELPRO Papers: Documents from the FBI's Secret Wars Against Dissent in the United States,* wrote: "The local police, prosecutors and the FBI in their effort to destroy the Rainbow Coalition and other national radical groups secretly instructed its field offices to propose schemes to 'misdirect, discredit, disrupt and otherwise neutralize' specific individuals and groups. Final authority rested with top FBI officials in Washington, who demanded assurance that 'there is no possibility of embarrassment to the Bureau.' More than 2,000 individual actions were approved."

In a memo, the FBI directly identified the Young Patriots as an ally of the Chicago Chapter of the Black Panthers. They pulled out all the stops to destroy alliances between the Panthers, street gangs such as the Mau Maus, and just about anyone who might listen to the vision of the Panthers.

Besides the FBI and its hirelings were other agencies that had no budget estimates, although we may fairly suppose that the black-ops pros of the National Security Agency, the CIA, the army intelligence, the Civil Service Commission, and the Department of Health, Education and Welfare did not work for free. In addition to the federal agencies were the municipal police "Red Squads" that were operating in every major city in the country. The Chicago Red Squad was running as many as 500 agents (143 in New York, 84 in Los Angeles, and 40 in Boston).

Under the terms of COINTELPRO, all of these agencies — federal and municipal — were supposed to be coordinating their work with the FBI.

The FBI targeted the Black Panther Party, Students for a Democratic Society, the Young Lords and the Young Patriots as a "formidable threat," as described in FBI memos obtained by the Freedom of Information Act. A memo dated May 1, 1969, from Hoover to the Chicago office of the FBI Counter Intelligence Program, states: "Authority is granted to instruct selected BPP informants for use in creating a rift between the BPP and the Students for a Democratic Society."

The 1969 memo continues:

Chicago has proposed that BPP informants be instructed to plant the idea that SDS is exploiting the BPP. There are various good arguments available to accomplish this, such as the SDS is using the BPP for their dirty work or SDS will relegate the BPP to the status of servants. The planting of these ideas in the minds of the BPP leaders should pose no problems. It would be a definite advantage if these two groups were alienated. We are authorizing Chicago to instruct selected informants to plant ideas and cautioning them to make sure that various ideas are different in nature and, of course, will not leave BPP leaders with the idea that this is a plan.

An additional memo to the Director of the FBI from the Counterintelligence Program in Chicago specifically targets the Young Patriots and the Young Lords. It states: "In recent weeks also, the local BPP group effected a similar coalition with the Young Lords, a near north side Puerto Rican youth gang and the Young Patriots, the latter an off-shoot of Job or Income Now (JOIN), an SDS affiliate group of young whites. Chicago will follow this and related developments closely and, as the opportunity presents itself, will submit appropriate counterintelligence suggestions."

The FBI also tried to recruit members of the Patriots. In 1969, Bobby McGinnis, Ronnie Reuss and I were invited to Augustana College in Rock Island, Illinois to make a presentation on the Young Patriots at a screening of the "American Revolution II," a recent documentary about the coalition between the Illinois Black Panthers and the Young Patriots. That evening we were invited to a student's house for a party. Around midnight, we left the party to return to Chicago. Shortly after leaving, we were stopped and surrounded by several police vehicles, ordered out, and to lay face down in the road. Our vehicle was searched, and we were arrested for possession of stolen property and suspicion of having a controlled substance.

The cops said that during the vehicle search they found two collector coins belonging to the student that lived in the house that we just left, in addition to a white powder. We stated that we were not guilty, and did not know anything about the items found in the car. Although we did plead guilty for having open alcohol, we were not charged with that crime. We were handcuffed and arrested. Then it became obvious that it was some kind of a set-up.

Because it was a weekday, we expected to go to court and be arraigned. Instead, each of one was taken individually into an interrogation room, where we were met with two FBI agents. We were told that we were facing jail time for stolen property, and more years would be added when the results of the suspicious powered substance returned. Eventually, they stated that if we were to become their informants, then all charges would be dropped, and there would be a financial gain. They also stated that the vehicle that we had borrowed was being impounded, because its owner David Komatsu had recently traveled to Cuba. They explained that even though the vehicle did not go to Cuba, it's possible that it was used for drug trafficking due to the suspicious white power found in it. We knew that the ordeal was bullshit, so we refused to cooperate or accept their offer.

When our lawyer arrived and heard of the FBI's attempts to recruit us as informants, and the physical evidence against us, he threatened to file false arrest and harassment charges against the FBI and the police. To our surprise, all charges were dropped, and we were released. But the cops still couldn't determine what the suspicious white powder was. Mr. Komatsu informed Bertucci that it was flea powder for his dog!

In May of 1969, members of the Rainbow Coalition were again trying to defend themselves. Mayor Daley and Illinois States Attorney Edward Hanrahan announced that a "War on Gangs" program would be launched to rid the city of gangs that were a threat to the safety of the citizens of Chicago. Not coincidentally, this act came with the help of COINTELPRO, and was announced only days after the Rainbow Coalition and the Young Lords attempted to march on Daley's Bridgeview neighborhood protesting the murder of the Young Lords' Manuel Ramos. Furthermore, it was only days after the premier of "American Revolution II." Daley's police stopped the marchers from entering his neighborhood with full riot gear.

The Daley Machine kept people separated by its perverse system of racism. The mayor was very satisfied if gangs, poor ethnic and minority groups, and people of color were fighting each other, as long as they stayed in their "place," were unseen, and did not cross into middle and upper class communities or stayed with their own race. Dissension gave the machine the excuse to convince residents that the city's unlawful orders to the Chicago Police to use excessive force was not only necessary but legal. A terrified population meant a healthy defense budget for the Daley Machine.

This task could be implemented by convincing the public that the Rainbow Coalition, dissident groups and gangs, who disagreed with the machine's dictator, were criminals and needed to be feared. The more statistics the city could gather on violence by these groups, gangs and communities meant more federal and state money the city could appropriate for the police. In Chicago's ghetto, Daley did not want laws to be obeyed, because obeying the law was not profitable.

Undoubtedly, Daley knew how to deal with street gangs. But what he was facing was his worst enemy — highly visible, radical and racially diverse organizations, whose membership included many former gang members that were now political activist and who understood the community's needs better than he did. His old group, the Hamburgs, were only interested in advancing power to white people. Even the name Rainbow Coalition, representing all races, became a threat to Daley's power in Chicago. This revolutionary coalition spoke with the same voice, and acted as one group, even as each organization remained autonomous in its decision-making. Daley was determined to stop it from gaining any political power in Chicago.

In 1969, there were 452 gangs operating in Chicago. Daley's concern was that if they would be brought into the Rainbow Coalition, or otherwise unite, he would lose most of his power to control the city. Daley, Hanrahan, and members of the Red Squad and COINTELPRO went on a campaign to criminalize street gangs and the Rainbow Coalition. Daley declared that:

"They extort money from businessmen and school children. They are responsible for assault, rape, robbery, burglary, and murder. By their actions, they seek to terrorize the community for the sole purpose of personal enrichment. Their actions indicate that they have no regard for their community or its residents, but are interested only in their personal gain. They seek to cloak this criminal activity under the guise of social involvement and what they advertise as constructive endeavors. Unfortunately, some groups which have no real knowledge of the community disregard the record and are misled into supporting criminal-led gangs."

We were sure that Daley's statement referring to gangs "cloaking criminal activities under the guise of social involvement" referred to members of the Rainbow Coalition. There were criminally-led gangs in Chicago, but they were not members of the Rainbow Coalition. The Rainbow Coalition member groups were radical community organizations. During the initial organizational stages of the Rainbow Coalition, other gangs were approached to join, such as the Black Stone Rangers, Cobras and others. Most sympathized with our purpose but declined. The Young Patriots found it interesting that the accusations that gangs were guilty of extortion, assault, rape, robbery, burglary and murder were exactly what members of the Chicago police department were being accused of having committed in the past.

On June 7, 1969, the Panthers responded to the "War on Gangs" in their newspaper. In an article titled "Pig Daley to Destroy So Called Gangs," they wrote:

(Daley) and his mad dog capitalist conspirators are plotting to murder potential revolutionary brothers and sisters who are to be true representatives of the oppressed communities. These brothers and sisters are poor just like you and I. They are poor and sometimes confused, not because they choose to be; but because the so-called representatives in Washington DC, Springfield, Illinois, the so-called representatives in city hall sit around on their fat asses and talk about conditions, and never do a damn thing about them ... The real gang that creates violence is the Pig Daley's gang.

On July 1, 1969, Commander of the Chicago Red Squad William Olson testified before a senate subcommittee that the Black Panthers were a major threat to the citizens of Chicago and the United States. He again indicated from an FBI memo, without naming the groups, that the Black Panthers had recruited similar groups among Puerto Rican and poor white radicals who support them.

Due to the media coverage in Chicago and suburban areas, both Daley's and Olson's statements had a profound effect on the number of visitors to Uptown. Financial contributions to community organizations dropped, and the number of outside volunteers participating in those programs dropped. Also, the Rainbow Coalition faced more harassment from the Chicago police. There was a notable increase in surveillance by plain-clothes officers in unmarked police vehicles, more intense questioning, and threats while being stopped by the police, in addition to our apartments being raided at all hours of the night.

Other Uptown groups, such as the Uptown Area People's Planning Coalition, experienced more harassment, with the police stopping and threatening their members. Roger Willis — a young community resident from West Virginia who was not a member but sympathized with us — was targeted, harassed, and identified as a Young Patriots member by the cops, as well as other non-members. The cops believed that all Uptown youth were potential members, and discouraged them from joining us.

The Young Lords and Black Panthers also experienced more harassment. Gangs in other neighborhoods also felt the effects of the "War on Gangs." The Thorndale Jag Offs, a gang north of Uptown, had several of their leaders arrested and sentenced to prison terms for what they said were "false charges" ranging from theft to attempted murder.

In March of 1970, an article appeared in the Chicago Tribune newspaper that attempted to criminalize the Young Patriots. Titled "Police Seek to Link Loop Bomb, Raided Group," the article stated that the Chicago Police were attempting to link the Young Patriots in Chicago to a bomb that was discovered in the Chicago downtown building six months earlier. The article adds that the police had raided an apartment in the Lakeview community where several groups were attending a seminar on anarchy, and found floor plans of several Chicago buildings. The location of the bomb found six months earlier was marked with an "X" on one of the maps.

The article says that the police arrested a member of the Young Patriots, in addition to members of the Latin Cobras, Black Assassins and Black Disciples. The Young Patriots had no associations with any of these groups, and none of our members were present at the seminar. The article did not identify who wrote it, and when asked to produce evidence, the Chicago Tribune stated that they did not know how it got into their newspaper. We believed that the article was submitted by the FBI as part of their campaign to spread false news in accordance to one of their memos.

Even Republican Alderman Robert O'Rourke of Uptown's 48th Ward was involved in harassing street people who he considered gang members. He would go on ride-alongs with two police officers for his protection. O'Rourke and the two uniformed police officers stopped me as I was walking on Sheridan Road. He made it clear that he was there to serve justice on street gangs, and that he was going to rid Uptown of them. I informed him that the Young Patriots was not a gang but an organization to serve the community.

O'Rourke also stated that he knew that I was a student at Northeastern Illinois University and cautioned me about recruiting college students into the Young Patriots. After beating me on the legs with a night stick, searching me, and much verbal abuse by the cops, I was told to go back and tell my "gang" that they were coming after us. It was not unusual for Republican and Democratic politicians to agree with each other when it came to common enemies. Neither party liked us, considering us a threat to the stranglehold that they both had on the neighborhood. On August 11, 1970, O'Rourke sent the following letter to Mayor Daley:

Dear Mayor Daley,

A matter has just come to my attention that causes me concern, and I am not certain as to what procedure I should follow. I am, therefore, presenting the matter directly to you, as I know you will take whatever steps are necessary.

I am enclosing a Polaroid photo of a poster (indicating Daley to be the instigator of the riots during the Democratic Convention in Chicago) that is on the door of the Young Patriots organization located at 4408 North Sheridan Road. The organization, as you know, bears some watching. My, concern, however, is that some unbalanced person could be influenced by the poster.

Sincerely,

Robert J. O'Rourke, Alderman, 48th Ward

We had always feared that any member of the Young Patriots could be the next victim of police brutality or murder. John Howard was a Southern migrant and a member of JOIN from its very beginning. He was featured in the film "American Revolution II" trying to unite people in Uptown in support of the Black Panther-Young Patriots coalition. Raymond Tackett was associated with the Young Patriots, and was a member of Rising Up Angry, an affiliate group. Both Howard and Tackett returned to their homes in the South to organize using Rainbow politics. Both were killed because of their beliefs.

According to the Firing Line newspaper: "On a trip home to Georgia in 1969, he (John Howard) was recognized as 'the guy who loves niggers in Chicago.' He was found the next day with his throat cut. Raymond Tackett was killed in 1973 under circumstances eerily similar to John Howard's murder. Tackett returned to his home state of Kentucky to organize in the mining town of Evars. He was in the process of starting a Serve the People–inspired free clinic when he was killed.

But it was the Black Panthers and Young Lords who suffered the most repression by the Chicago Police. On December 4, 1969, head of the Chicago Chapter of the Black Panther Party Fred Hampton and Black Panther Party member Mark Clark were murdered by the Chicago Police Department in the early hours of the morning while they were sleeping. Hampton had been betrayed by one of his closest friends, who had become an informant. Over 90 shots were fired by the police, with only one fired into the wall by the Black Panthers. Later studies showed that the single bullet was believed to be fired by Clark, and probably in self-defense, as it was fired in an upward direction.

While Fred Hampton and several members of Panthers were in Canada, informant William O'Neal, a member of the Black Panther Party and a friend of Fred Hampton, was instructed by Roy Mitchell of the FBI to get a detailed floor plan of Hampton's apartment, located at 2337 Monroe St., for a planned police raid. The floor plans were turned over to Richard Jalovec, assistant to Illinois State Attorney Edward Harahan, who passed the information on to the chief of a special prosecutor's unit.

Fred Hampton was a visionary and believed that street gangs should stop waging war against each other. He was the primary source for getting the Young Patriots and Young Lords, along with the Black Panthers, to form the Rainbow Coalition. His belief was that gangs needed to channel their energy into serving their community. He knew that his dream of a rainbow coalition of people could work for the benefit of all, but it would be a struggle, because the gangs have been fighting each other for so long. Racism would have no place in Hampton's dream. Class struggle by all people overcoming their oppression was his revolutionary dream.

The murder of Hampton and Clark was devastating to

the Rainbow Coalition. The members of the Young Patriots felt that a great friend and leader had been taken from them. Hampton felt the pain of all poor people, regardless of their color, and he knew first-hand the suffering caused by poverty, racism and class hatred. He wanted to help all people to gain power so the they could unite and fight for equality in a system that denied it to them.

We were in hopes that another leader would take over that had the same compassion and caring that he had. Our concern was that given we were Southerners, we would not be allowed to continue our partnership with the Black Panthers. The Young Patriots resolved that we would continue working under the umbrella of the Rainbow Coalition if Hampton was replaced with someone who shared his political beliefs and is willing to continue working with us. We wanted to continue our relationship with the Young Lords, too. We hoped the Black Panthers would continue to do the same.

Splits and New Realities

any of the articles and recordings of the Young Patriots center around one of our members William "Preacherman" Fesperman. He served as Minister of Information of the Young Patriots for a while. He informed our Central Committee that he was attempting to organize a national Young Patriots party. Fesperman had been in Uptown for a short period of time. He moved from North Carolina to study theology in Chicago.

In 1968, Peggy Terry and I met Preacherman at the Southern Christian Leadership Conference's Resurrection City in Washington DC. He was a seminary student and professed an interest in working with the Young Patriots and poor Southern whites. We invited him to visit Uptown. Shortly afterwards, he moved his family to Uptown, and began to work with the Patriots. He possessed good oratory skills and shared our revolutionary beliefs. He represented the group at various speaking engagements.

After the murder of Fred Hampton, he proposed that due to the accomplishments and progress of the national student and other movements, it was time for us to move into the national movement, maintaining that to continue to organize in Uptown only was trivial. He stated that other Patriots members felt that it was time to go national. We disagreed with him, because we were convinced that we hadn't built a solid enough base in Chicago yet. To concentrate on a national program would weaken all accomplishments that had been made due to us finally having a voice in the community.

Many Young Patriots members resented the outsiders, scholars, students, politicians and members of the national movement attempting to advise us on organizing and conducting programs that they knew nothing about. Many outsiders didn't understand the culture of the community and were not aware that the definition of self-determination was paramount to us. Outsiders could leave when they wanted to, but community residents could not. The Young Patriots had grown, and we learned more than the outsiders, who initially taught us organizing techniques. We did not have time to teach other outsiders, especially as most of our time and energy was spent in battles with "Urban Renewal," police brutality, and daily survival.

We believed that revolution needed time and community resistance to be proven workable. Poor people would fight battles of their own choosing, in their own community, and establish their own programs before going national. Preacherman disagreed and went on to establish the Patriot Party, with chapters in New York, Washington DC, Oregon, and New Haven Connecticut, claiming that the split from the Young Patriot Organization was amicable.

On February 17, 1970, an article titled "The Patriot Party Speaks to the Movement" appeared in the West Coast Black Panther newspaper. Written by Preacherman, the article made slanderous remarks about the Young Patriot Organization in Chicago:

The Patriot Party grew out of the old Young Patriot Organization in Uptown Chicago. We split from the Young Patriot Organization because they were more concerned with old friendships, individuals, rather than the masses of people in Uptown. They would rather be friends with a few people and indulge in drinking than listening to the community's cry for help. Those old friends were holding the Patriot Party back. The Patriot Organization was guilty of extreme liberalism. For the sake of peace and friendship, things have clearly gone wrong. A few programs were started by YPO in Uptown Chicago. However, people were not being educated to the struggle, so they had the effect of being reformist programs.

Responding to the article, Young Patriots Chairman

Bobby McGinnis said that "Fesperman was forced to leave Uptown by members of the Young Patriot Organization, because of his blusterous ego and refusal to conform to the needs of the Uptown people. He was more interested in gaining a national reputation and an identity with other radical and revolutionary groups than serving the needs of Uptown." While he was representing the Patriot Party, he was recruiting support for a national party, and did not make the Young Patriots aware until he proposed the move to a national organization. His article was received as a retaliation for being forced to leave Uptown.

Bobby McGinnis and the Patriots Central Committee added that: "The split between Fesperman and YPO was not agreeable or negotiable." Also, the statement expressed that the Patriot Party and any chapters established were only "chapters in training," and demanded they discontinue the use of the original Eleven Point program, and develop their own to fit their party platform.

Also, the Young Patriots saw the need to address the Confederate Flag, which was worn by many Patriot Party members because the Young Patriots in Chicago had discontinued its use. We had grown in our knowledge of the civil war, and it had become clear to us that the South was the counterrevolutionary and reactionary side in the conflict. In our view, there was no justification for any revolutionary group using a symbol of racists. The flag represented a system of slaveocracy, which not only perpetuated the slavery of Blacks, but also the powerlessness of poor whites, to further racial and class hatred. We believed that the so-called "rebel" flag continued to offend our Black brothers and sisters, because it was a symbol of hate from a period in history in which they were nothing more than private property to be bought and sold.

The Patriots response was sent to the Black Panther Paper, but we received no response of it appearing in any of their publications. In our defense, we may have been a little bit guilty of all of the allegations, and most likely so were some members of the Patriot Party. It is wrong to assume that because one joins an organization, that a transformation instantly occurs, and one becomes completely indoctrinated into the beliefs and purpose of the organization. Educating takes time. Old friends would have to be given time to grow and learn in the organization.

We were street people. We did frequent bars and pool halls, as we did before we became a political organization. Fesperman too was known to visit bars while wearing the Confederate Flag to discuss the needs of the community while drinking with local residents. To change our community, we would meet people on their own turf. Sometime that would be in bars, while other times in the street, or at community action meetings. Our actions spoke for themselves. We did drink, smoke weed, and experimented with recreational drugs, as did members of the national movement.

We would talk with people who frequented bars,

because that was where we knew how to contact them for community activities and protests. And yes, Fesperman was correct, we did hang out with "old friends and drinking buddies," because many were trying to navigate through life's problems (poverty, sickness and depression), while others possessed organizing skills (in coal mining, for example) that were helpful to us. Also, this is where we would learn about their needs and get them involved. Sometime the greatest act is to help pull someone from the bottom of a bottle.

We were respected in bars, the streets and community action meetings, because we offered a solid program through the Eleven Point program. We did not change to satisfy the politicians, liberals, conservatives and opportunists. We were about revolution, and the community understood that our goal was to make Uptown a self-determined community, run by the people. We were not saints or pacifist when we had to defend our community, and would fight if we were challenged.

There were organizational disagreements between the Chicago Young Patriots and the newly formed Patriot Party about who should lead the Rainbow Coalition. In an article in the New York Times, titled "Black Panthers Join Coalition with Puerto Rican and Appalachian Groups," a quote attributed to Defense Captain of the Patriot Party Arthur Turco caused dissent between the Young Patriot Organization and the Patriot Party. The article notes:

"Since the Panthers and the Young Lords are the best organized of the groups and that the Blacks are the largest oppressed element in American society. Mr. Turco sees the black group as the leaders of the coalition."

We felt that Turco's statement went against the original purpose of the Rainbow Coalition, because to allow any group or individual to lead the Coalition would eliminate self-determination, and the Coalition would become just another movement organization controlled by a hierarchy. The Rainbow Coalition was a code word for solidarity. The Patriot Party had forgotten that the coalition was not under the control of any leader, but rather each member organization had equal representation. We viewed this as an attempt to highjack the coalition and make the original coalition irrelevant. Further, the Young Patriots in Chicago were very well organized.

The Patriot Party continued organizing nationally with free health clinics, food pantries and drug abuse programs. Their efforts were short-lived because their leadership was not prepared for the repression of the FBI and the police. After a short period of time, residents in their targeted communities did not trust the outsiders. They were also reluctant to get involved due to fear of becoming victims of police brutality and harassment. Further, the party failed to build a base of community organizations and community leaders, and were attacked by racist groups who did have an established base in the communities. Several Patriot Party members were jailed on false charges, such as gun violations and drug charges.

According to a source who requested not to be identified: "Several women, including prostitutes, infiltrated the Patriot Party and some were police informants. Since they were new to the communities, there was no full proof way of identifying anyone's background and identity." The FBI also spread rumors in Black Chicago neighborhoods and communities that we were a front for the KKK and American Nazi Party. The Black Panthers and other groups in Chicago did not believe the rumors, and saw them as an attempt by the FBI to disrupt relations among Rainbow Coalition members.

Leader of the Eugene (Oregon) Chapter of the Patriot Party Chuck Armsbury was arrested on a gun violation and sentenced to ten years in federal prison. Armsbury, who was also a PhD student at the University of Oregon at Eugene, was well known and respected by students, and carried a lot of influence on campus. In court, a member of his chapter testified against him. He was part of a wave of arrests by the FBI and local police.

Armsbury stated at the time: "It seemed that the remaining leadership forgot about me. I made several attempts to contact them for help but it never came." Soon after Armsbury's arrest, all Patriot Party chapters were attacked by the FBI and local cops, and began to disband. Soon after the sweep, many members left the party, including Fesperman, who lived in seclusion from the movement. He passed away from cancer in his state of North Carolina.

Further controversy arose after Fesperman left Uptown and founded the Patriot Party. And it is still a point of contention today: Who actually founded the Rainbow Coalition? The first contact between the Panthers and Patriots, and some members of SDS, was in 1968, through the Peace and Freedom Party (PFP). The PFP asked for a representative from Uptown to be the running mate for the Eldridge Cleaver for President campaign. Peggy Terry, who broke from a family tradition of Klan membership, took on the task as his Vice Presidential running mate. The Patriots and some SDS students took on the task of running Terry's campaign.

In 1968, Field Secretary of the Chicago Chapter of the Black Panther Party Bobby Lee caught the interest of the Patriots while attending a community council meeting of mostly middle-class, white liberals, who began to scold members of the Patriots for not working to get out of poverty, after making an appeal for financial help to run their programs. Lee was quick to defend the white Patriots members, met with them after the meeting, and agreed to come to Uptown. Lee reported to Fred Hampton about his experience with white anti-racist Hillbillies, who were teaching revolutionary politics in Uptown, and suggested that the Panthers form a relationship with us.

Hampton agreed that a relationship was needed, and was worth the risk to fight segregation in Chicago. Lee reported back to the Patriots, and a community meeting was organized to solidify the partnership. Lee was named chairman of the police brutality committee, and a community meeting with the district police commander was held to inform him that police brutality would no longer be tolerated. The Patriots began adopting some of the Panthers' programs and ideology. This was the beginning of the relationship with the Chicago Chapter of the Black Panther Party for Self Defense.

Here is the controversy about who actually founded the Rainbow Coalition. On April 4, 1969, a meeting took place with Fred Hampton and Bobby Lee from the Black Panther Party, Jose (Cha Cha) Jimenez of the Young Lords Organization, and Bill (Preacherman) Fesperman of the Young Patriots Organization, who were said to be the only founders of the First Rainbow Coalition. I am not qualified to speak for the Black Panther Party or the Young Lords Organization, but I am qualified to speak for the Young Patriot Organization, as I am a founding member and was an active member at the time of the meeting.

Fesperman has been identified as the founder and leader of the Patriots. He was neither. He became the spokesperson of the organization because of his communication skills. He was assigned to attend the April 4 meeting only to represent the Patriots, and report back to the central committee. He, along with the central committee, agreed to participate. Therefore, the entire Patriots central committee were the actual co-founders of the Rainbow Coalition, and they began identifying themselves as such. The decision was easily made due to the Patriots' past relationship with the Panthers by way of the Cleaver-Terry Campaign, as well as their relationship with Bobby Lee.

Later Fesperman detached from the Chicago Patriots and founded the Patriot Party, working closely with the National Black Panther Party.

The End of the Young Patriots

It was after the Chicago City Council approved construction of the proposed city college, and all necessary federal agencies were in agreement — in addition to COINTELPRO — that the Young Patriots saw their final days. The construction of the college was long and tedious, and many of the vacant buildings sat empty for long periods of time before they were demolished.

Truman College opened its doors in 1976, taking up a quarter of Uptown's residential area. The Young Patriots organizing base was literally wiped out in a matter of a few months. It was futile to try to organize. The Southern migrant was once again sent out on the migrant trail. Many went back South to eke out whatever living they can. Some moved on to other cities, while other turned to alcohol and stayed in Chicago, blending into the street

174

environment of so many winos and drunks.

There was a small portion that had been able to find jobs and become financially stable — they stayed in Uptown and continue to live there today. By 1975, the destruction of the residential community ended any hopes of continuing to organize white migrants. Many members of the Young Patriots became migrants also. Some moved to Tennessee, California, Alabama, Kentucky, West Virginia, Baltimore and New York, and some to other Illinois and Wisconsin cities.

The Southern Cultural Exchange Center attempted to organize groups to represent the community, with plans that would remove residents in the Truman target area, but were ignored by the Daley Machine. All attempts by other activist groups to have influence on decisions for the community were also ignored. The city had won, and plans were put into play to rid Uptown of all poor people, returning the area to the affluence of the past.

For safety reasons, I had removed myself from many activities with the exception of attending Northeastern Illinois University Uptown Center to continue my education, while still being engaged in organizing in Uptown. After graduation in 1973, I was hired to be a public relations and community representative and co-lecturer for Northeastern, which gave me the opportunity to expand the university's programs to recruit poor residents. Then, after leaving NEIU in 1975, I accepted a short-term job in the Model City Program working with senior citizen and handicapped programs. The program director was from a working-class background, and thought we would make a great team.

After I accepted a job at the Montrose Urban Progress Center in Uptown, my employment was terminated after nine months, due to falsifying information to get needed services and motorized wheelchairs to a few individuals who had been denied services. But perhaps the best reason was that while I worked there, I had gained access to information of the Democratic Party's plans, proposals and decisions for the community. I would advise block clubs and opposing organizations of the Machine's plans, and literally kill Daley's efforts before they even started. After being exposed, I was fired and again targeted by the Chicago police.

In 1977, legendary Chicago folk singer Mick Scott and I organized "Blues to Bluegrass," an organization that recruited progressive and revolutionary musicians from the Chicago area to help their community by performing for schools, block clubs, nursing homes, and doing benefits for community organizations. At the same time, Blues to Bluegrass would expose new and existing talent, and build an audience for them. Mick Scott and Bill Cody would recruit musicians, and I would advertise for them and book them into local venues and other gigs, such as parties, schools, etc.

While performing benefits, they would get a percentage of the door and free drinks. The regular commission would be collected from booking gigs, and it would be used for publicity and advertising for their upcoming gigs. Blues to Bluegrass was an organization made up of community organizations, musicians and other interested people, such as photographers, who donated their time. The group organized special low-cost music lessons for under-privileged children with the Old Town School of Folk Music and other musicians in Chicago. The program was a tremendous success, and continued for many years.

Rising Up Angry, the Southern Cultural Exchange Center, and many other organizations benefited from Blues to Bluegrass. By 1975-1976, the organization boasted over 150 artists. Recently, Blues to Bluegrass has been rebooted, and is actively involved in providing benefits and other cultural activities in Chicago and the South. I don't know of any wars that have been fought over music. Music is something that everybody can understand, no matter where they came from — it can really bring people together. That's why we called it Blues to Bluegrass, because it can be any kind of instrument or any style of vocals.

Music is the universal language that speaks to the struggles of the people, and it is best expressed by the people who live in the community themselves. Artists subjected to the pressures of Nashville, New York or Los Angeles are not always in the best position to reflect the needs and desires of the community, particularly the hard, cold reality of daily life. Music can sometime be a key element to commonality, and can help tremendously in bringing different groups together to work on a common cause.

Our earliest band was the "Special Consensus Bluegrass Band," which has won many musical awards, and still contributes to the community. Mike Dunbar, KoKo Taylor, Eddie Clearwater were among the many who donated their talents. Our thinking was that it was time that organizations and people start promoting themselves, instead of some big company which doesn't give a damn about the people in their community. The belief was that if we could take one person or band and make them famous, they can come back and do benefits for organizations who serve people in need. It was an important way to raise money, because it expressed the people's identity.

Going Back Home, Feeling Like A Fugitive

I'm on my way back home again
to the air, the grass, the trees
and with the help of this old Ford
I'll be home by three
The Windy City just ain't my bag
It kicked me in the ass.
— LARRY GILES, SOUTHERN MIGRANT

n 1978, my wife, daughter and I relocated back to my hometown Dayton, Tennessee. The first week back I encountered police harassment, when I was pulled over by a Rhea County police officer. I knew it was not only because my car had Illinois license plates. The officer knew who I was, and asked me how long I intended on staying in town. This was only the first of many times that I would be stopped and asked the same question.

My sister Geraldine informed me that a year before I came back home, the county sheriff and the United States Postal Service Postmaster visited her to inquire about several movement newspapers that I had sent her. They advised her that this was subversive, and to refuse any other deliveries. She stated that she had not received any in years, and that they had no right to tell her what she could or could not read. The authorities also visited my mother, inquiring about several handguns that went missing while my brother Ralph was working on the truck docks in Chicago — both of us were involved in JOIN at the time.

I literally could not find employment in the entire county. However, within a few days of our arrival in Tennessee, my wife did find employment in the Dayton Housing Authority assisting the director Wallace Rice, who was the former juvenile judge that was primarily responsible for falsely sentencing many to jail terms. While doing some filing, she discovered a confidential file marked "Thurman Family," containing FBI information on my brothers and sisters, with specific information about me and my brother Ralph. When she asked Rice about the file, he ignored her. Not being familiar with the politics of a small town, she was very scared for the well-being of our daughter. We started making plans to leave.

By coincidence, and within a week of my wife discovering the file, a friend who was close to the local police informed me that the cops were making plans to arrest me. Within a few days, we left Tennessee with just a few belongings, and moved to Georgia. We felt like fugitives on the run, yet we had done nothing wrong. In retrospect it all made sense: J. Edgar Hoover had classified the Black Panther Party as a threat to national security, and the Young Patriots were caught in that net due to their affiliation with the Rainbow Coalition. We were fortunate that we discovered this information before action was taken against us.

For many years, I wandered around the South, and on two occasions moved back to Chicago. During those years, I got a divorce and decided to stay in Illinois. During that time, I was employed by the Alternative Youth Agency in Chicago, as Director of School Base Services, to work with at-risk high school students and on gang intervention. I lived in a Northwest suburb, and would travel to and from work each day, being very careful not to be in Uptown at night.

In 1995, I also volunteered for the Wayside Cross Ministries Homeless Center in Elgin, Illinois. Later, I took up a part-time work organizing computerized learning centers for the men in residency program, as well as for a shelter for battered women and children in Aurora, Illinois. Both Alternatives and Wayside were great opportunities for raising awareness for social change. I encouraged the women and the residents to look at alternatives for their life. The major success was many residents learned computer skills, and many completed their GED.

After my job was completed with Wayside Cross Ministries, I had remarried and entered into the world of retail automotive sales, in which I spent the next twenty years. This was not the career that I wanted, but it was all I could find due to a major slump in the economy. The social services field had been saturated with people with higher educational degrees, including in entry positions. Because most social service agencies had become non-profits, they had to conform to mandates of their funders, and that left few openings for those with lower education.

My Bachelor of Arts university degree was useless. I believe that my involvement in the movement prevented me from being hired for many positions, although I had impeccable qualifications. On February 25, 2014, I applied for a gun owner's permit in Alabama, and was denied due to two arrests that should have been expunged. They were a disorderly conduct charge in Chicago when I was seventeen and the stolen property charge in Rock Island, Illinois, which was dropped from my record. Both charges were, however, part of a federal record, and they appear when I have a background check. After sending requests for affidavits to the City of Chicago and Rock Island County, Illinois, I received affidavits stating that no records existed of my arrests, and I was granted a gun owner's permit.

Rebooting the Rainbow

n October of 2010, I relocated to Alabama. In 2015, due to not being involved in the national movement, I was surprised to discover that many people wanted to know about the Young Patriots Organization. Two books had been published that gave accurate accounts of our work: "Hillbilly Nationalists, Urban Race Rebels, Black Power: Community Organizing in Radical Times" by Amy Sonnie and James Tracy and "From the Bullet to the Ballot" by Jakobi Williams. Filmmaker Ray Santisteban was working on a new documentary about the original Rainbow Coalition. With this information and a desire to organize again, I decided to reboot the Young Patriot Organization with the knowledge of the original Young Patriots and the original Rainbow Coalition.

I believe that if the original Rainbow Coalition continued, it would have been a major force in Chicago and the nation, by uniting thousands of poor people who usually fought each other and providing a model of how best to organize and gain power. Some believed it could have become a major third party. In spite of the murders, brutality and state oppression, the idea of the coalition did catch on. The successful elections of Harold Washington as the first black mayor of Chicago and Bobby Rush to State Senate and Congress both employed an organizing model inspired by the Rainbow Coalition.

I could start with a clean slate, now that both Daley and Hoover, as well as my other adversaries, were deceased. I could start by uniting college student and poor white communities with other racial and minority groups, preaching revolutionary change and socialism, which still pose a threat to the status quo. The coalition in the past either had to be controlled or destroyed. I strongly believe that the Rainbow Coalition and the Young Patriots model can be as effective today as it was in the past.

The Young Patriots Organization has continued organizing, and has seven chapters across the country. Their activism has been directly responsible for the creation of the Homeless Construction Coalition in Alabama. They have also partnered with many progressive groups to organize the poor and homeless, and to get immigrant detainees hearings and services.

Most of the hard work of organizing is letting people know who you are and what you want, while inspiring their involvement. History has a way of offering a blueprint of the past for people to follow in the present day. Many of the young activists have never heard of the Patriots or the original Rainbow Coalition. Most people today are familiar with the Rainbow Coalition that is related to Jesse Jackson's Rainbow Push Coalition and his presidential campaign.

To get my organizing started, I had to create a Young Patriot mission statement, which read as follows: "To find, support, inspire, offer resources and train residents of poor and working-class communities to become leaders in the policies that effect their daily lives by building upon the accomplishments of the original Young Patriots and the Original Rainbow Coalition. We will carry out our mission by direct contact with grassroots community groups to offer them a model to build (in many areas interracial coalitions)."

We also created a new Seven Point program:

1. SELF-DETERMINATION, INEQUALITY AND RACISM: *Dedicated to overcoming racism and sexism, support ongoing struggles of poor, working-class peoples and immigrants for peace and human rights, end discrimination of all kinds and weaken materialism and dispel homophobia.*

2. EDUCATION: *All be given the same quality of education regardless of class status, all to be allowed to study their culture and heritage, stoppage of the school-to-prison pipeline.*

3. GENTRIFICATION: *To support grassroots organizations*

*and individuals who fight gentrification of their neighborhoods.
Housing for the poor and working-class people being moved by
gentrification.*

4. PRISONS: *Demand an end to privatization of prisons.
End to the "War on Drugs." Free all political prisoners and the
relocation of mentally-ill prisoners to mental health facilities,
end the school-to-prison pipeline.*

5. POLICE BRUTALITY: *End police brutality of all people,
[establish] citizen control of the police. Police must be from the
community that they serve.*

6. FOOD, HOUSING, HEALTHCARE: *All people are entitled to food, clothing, housing and healthcare for their survival.
Demand that the government ends its war on the poor, demand
that vacant properties such as strip malls, vacant houses and
warehouses be used for housing for the homeless and those living
under the economic poverty level, health services to be provided
to everyone.*

7. LABOR: *All people have a right to make a living, demand
that the government invest in jobs and job training to allow
everyone a decent income.*

In mid-2019, I was having a conversation with Candy
Ballanger, a long-time community activist in Huntsville,
Alabama. She asked a very important question: "If you
had just one wish, what do you think is the most important action to be taken to further the movement?" After a
brief thought and discussion, my response was that over
my many years of organizing, I have witnessed organizers

and organizations fall apart due to a lack of direction. I said, "they just seem to fizzle out and after a short period of time."

After actions, demonstrations and protests, people go their own separate way, and very little follow-up is done to organize them, refer them to other organizations, or form meaningful coalitions. Organizers sometimes just don't have enough interest, training or skills to hold the participants together. Many organizations don't know where to put them, or have the time and money to train them. I felt that the movement should have a vehicle to answer retention problems, in order to bring organizers and community residents together to enhance organizing skills and to develop new organizers.

Candi and I began talking with other community organizers, community leaders and residents, and within a couple of weeks, a school was born. In December of 2019, we named the school the "North Alabama School for Organizers (NASO)." We developed a moto, vision, purpose and mission following the legacy of the Rainbow Coalition.

MOTTO: Educate to Organize

VISION: To create a learning and educational environment to educate to organize — a school where people can attend to enhance and explore meaningful areas of organizing to empower themselves and their communities to be self-determined, solve problems, create change and control their own destiny.

PURPOSE: To train organizers, individuals and groups to take progressive action to strive for a better world through classes, hands-on experiences of projects and activities — to encourage the participants to strengthen their organization and take action to control their destiny.

MISSION: The North Alabama School for Organizers seeks to empower through intersectional education and training to form coalitions that take progressive actions toward progressive change.

Conclusion

The best way to identify the poor is to allow them to identify themselves. Much has been written about the dispossessed, but less has been written by the dispossessed themselves. Conventional wisdom, one would think, would lead more academics and scholars to encourage the 45-plus million living below the poverty line in the United States to write more, and encourage them to express their opinions about their life conditions. But that has failed.

Coming from a very poor and under-educated background, I have found that most poor people do not understand the rhetoric in much the intellectual writings, art and speech of those who confess to be experts on the lives of impoverished people. Not that the poor are completely illiterate and ignorant. To the contrary, one cannot assume that everyone understands and interprets their rhetoric. One big mistake for the upper classes to become experts about the lives of the poor and how they think. Many of the disadvantaged will only tell the researchers part of the truth, until a large amount of trust is built between them.

When I was eighteen, I was hired by an anthropologist to interview young folks in Uptown. At separate times with the same participants, asking the same questions, we would be given different answers. Many times, my questions would be considered truth because of mistrust of outsiders.

Identifying the poor white Southerner as ignorant might allow for learning, but too often they are grouped together as being stupid, and that indicates an inability to learn. I was considered a backward person and white trash. No doubt some still see me as a Southern white as being such today.

Poor people must be looked upon as being an important part of society, and given the same equal rights and tangible opportunities that have been denied to them by mainstream society, such as healthcare, employment, decent salaries, services and respect that effect their daily lives, in addition to self-determination of their lives and their communities. Of mandatory importance is for society to stop treating all the poor as second-class citizens.

The Black Panthers, Young Lords and the Young

Patriots in the Rainbow Coalition did not seek recognition or advice from academics, but listened intently to the voices of the disadvantaged. Then, they set out on a journey to reeducate society and convince the poor that their voices mattered in the greater scheme of things, and successfully made them partners to change the oppressive capitalist system, which has kept them in a perpetual downward spiral of poverty.

Further, the poor and working class feel that many are talking above them. Ideas, opinions and structures in society are laid out without allowing the opinions of the poor. We must stop judging them. If we are to give the poor a fighting chance to change society, then they must be included and encouraged to develop their own leadership skills to lead other deprived people. Leftists must reeducate them as any other population, and then allow them to reeducate their people, while giving the poor credit for participating.

The poor possess a very unique set of skills that does not come from a classroom, but from the day-to-day struggles of navigating through waters of despair, pain and the occasional success that shape their existence. Their plight cannot and should not be explained away in intellectual rhetoric. Understanding society's outcasts can only be effectively achieved by allowing the poor to educate the masses, by understanding them and giving them the necessary tools to do so. Identifying one as ignorant allows for learning, but too often the poor are identified as stupid, and that indicates an inability to learn. Both terms are wrong, because the poor possesses learning abilities that society deems foreign to them.

The poor must not be overlooked, but rather engaged and convinced that they are important. Something tangible needs to be provided — survival programs in healthcare, employment and training, decent salary, and other services that affect their daily lives and are controlled by them. Of mandatory importance is for society to stop treating the poor and working class as a second class. Only then can change take place, because they possess the needed down-to-earth learning abilities that can allow them to lead the revolution.

Both Dr. Martin Luther King and the Black Panther Party did not seek the approval of the rich or middle class, but listened intently to the voices of the poor. Then, they set out to reeducate the poor and convince them that their voices mattered in the greater scheme of things, and successfully made them partners in changing the capitalist society that kept them in a downward spiral of poverty.

Looking at a hypothetical analogy: I worked in the automotive business for a long time and know something about automobile engines. I have worked in politics practically all of my life and know some about how it works. Our government, both on the local and national levels, works in a way similar to an automotive engine. If it is not tuned up and the oil changed on a regular basis, or if too much is added, it becomes sluggish and eventually stops working.

Oil is the lifeblood of an engine, but old oil will likely damage it. In my opinion, this is what has happened to our governments: Too much old oil (politicians) is a hazard and should be changed. New oil (young politicians) needs to be added to ensure that the engine operates properly. In 2019, many new young progressive politicians and women were elected due to the politics of the "old oil." They should be heard, supported and encouraged, because they are in touch with the people. The choice for the future lies within all of us to replace the damaged engine and the old oil, or suffer the consequences. And if they are going to serve the poor, then they must listen to their needs.

Power comes from the people. If we are to build a flock, we must stop the fighting and mud-slinging within our organizations. Stop worrying about who gets the credit for success and stop assigning blame for what we deem as failure. Remember, organizers are being watched and critiqued by the marginalized who they profess to serve. The poor may have a completely different understanding of behavior and customs that need to be respected.

Although some rules might sound trivial to an outsider, they could be very important to the poor. Never identify as being equal to any marginalized group, unless you come from or have been identified as being equal.

Be polite. Never take anything from the poor. Only give respect and never brag about giving. Return anything you borrow. Never take advantage of relationships. Stay away from controversy and disputes within the groups. Only offer advice when asked.

It is obvious that the present system of capitalism is not working for the vast majority of the population in the US. Many are working within the system to change it, with very little success. Until people realize that they are being treated like a dog that only gets scraps from their master's table, rise up against their oppressors, and demand to be treated like human beings, then and only then will change come. Revolution is the only solution to gain equality and freedom.

The 11-Point Program of the Young Patriots Organization

The 11-Point Program of the Young Patriots Organization was inspired by the 10-Point Program of the Black Panther Party for Self Defense. The YPO adapted it to reflect the specific needs of Southern poor white people while connecting to national liberation struggles.

1. CLASS

We see that the key is truly understanding and improving our situation is to truly understand the nature of class society. We see that in America and in the world that those who have money control those who do not. We feel that the wealth of the world should be shared equally among all people. The workers who are the masses of people produce the wealth and they should control it. We see that our allies are those who have nothing and our enemies are those who have too much.

2. WELFARE OF THE PEOPLE

We believe that all people are entitled to adequate food, clothing, shelter and medical care. We believe that businesses should not make a profit on the things that we need to survive. We demand decent and adequate housing at a low cost for poor people. We demand that mothers who want to raise their children in their own home be paid for this vital work.

3. PIGS AND PIG POWER STRUCTURE

We demand the end to pigs murdering and brutalizing our people. The pigs are the tool of the rich men. The pigs are in our community to protect the property of the robber-baron landlords.

4. SCHOOLS-EDUCATION

We understand that the main purpose of the educational system as it now stands is to make people fit smoothly into the capitalistic society. We understand that the children of poor people are trained to be poor people — the children of factory workers are trained to work in factories — the children of rich people are trained to take their parents places. The schools are run like prison because this society is a prison. We demand that all people have the opportunity to develop their abilities.

5. DRAFT

We oppose the draft because it means poor and working class men fight rich men's wars. We oppose imperialistic wars such as the war in Vietnam. We believe that all patriotic men and women should serve only in the army of liberation. Rich people can buy their way out of the draft, but poor and working class people have no choice. We demand that the old rich men who create the wars should fight them and that the young men should stay home and construct a new society.

6. UNIONS

The idea of unions was a good thing. But we still know that the majority of Americans work long hours under bad conditions for poor wages and never have nothing to show for it. We demand an end to discrimination on the job and in the union. Men and women of all races should get equal wages and better working conditions. Unions claim to represent their members, but actually they represent union officials and sell their members down the river. Sell-out unions must be destroyed, therefore we support the right of workers to organize outside of the union. We realize that real change in this country will not happen until the people control their factories. When the workers control their factories they have no need for union representatives to bargain with the company.

7. EXPLOITATION OF THE COMMUNITY

We understand that the businessmen in the community make their living off of us. We understand that we make the products that they sell back to us. We demand that if businessmen intend to stay in the community, those profits be interested in the community in the form of goods and services.

8. RACISM

Racism is a tool of capitalism to make the people fight among themselves instead of fighting together for their freedom. Divisions of race and sex serve the interests of the rich ruling class and not of the people.

9. RELEASE ALL POLITICAL PRISONERS

We demand the release of all political prisoners. We understand that the majority of so-called "criminals" in our concentration camp prisons are victims of our class society. Justice is a luxury that only rich men can afford. There people should be released to build a new society instead of hidden away for society's mistakes.

10. CULTURAL NATIONALISM

We believe that to fight only for the interests of your close cultural brothers and sisters is not in the interest of all the people, and in fact perpetuates racism. We understand that our struggle is a class struggle. All power to the poor and working people! Cultural nationalism does not solve the political problems of the oppressed peoples, but only perpetuates exploitations. Capitalism makes millions on love-beads, afro-shorts and cowboy hats. Cultural nationalism is a tool of capitalist exploitation.

11. REVOLUTIONARY SOLIDARITY

Revolutionary solidarity with all oppressed people of this and all other countries and races defeats the divisions created by the narrow interests of cultural nationalism. We support all wars of national liberation and demand an immediate end to the war in Vietnam. Monopoly capitalism and corrupt Russian socialism are enemies of the oppressed peoples throughout the world.

Acknowledgements

I wish to thank the following people who without their help this book would not have been possible.

Antonio Lopez, Andy Keniston, Bobby McGinnis, Colleen Wessel McCoy, Myles Wessel-McCoy Carol Blakely, Bob Rehak, Bobby Lee, Elizabeth Jesse, Henry(Poison) Gaddis, Jacobi Williams, Jon Langford, Jose Jeminez Young Lords, Kristian Williams, Margi Devoe, Mike James, Marilyn Katz, Ralph Thurman, Roger Guy, Scott Crow, Billy Keniston, Ted Stein, Stan Mckinney, Illinois Black Panther Party Patrick Sturgus, Bob Lawson, Helen Schiller, Anndrena Belcher, Johnny Lester, Roger Willis, and Daniel Tucker.

A special thanks to Dr. Robert Brinkman, Carol Blakely and Chuck Armsbury for being a life time Young Patriot and comrade and someone that I could always count on to help me sort the history of YPO and for being great friends. Martin Billheimer and Jon Langford for being a great encourager and for recording songs from the Young Patriot songbook. Andy Willis for his great political discussions and his band the Amores for recording our songs. Ray Santisteban for allowing me to assist in the making of the First Rainbow Coalition documentary Rob Rehak for allowing me to use some pictures from his book Uptown: Portrait of a Chicago Neighborhood in the Mid 1970`s.

Nancy Hollander for the use her use of her historical photo of "Civilians Must Control Their Police." Paul Seigel and Maryann Majors in Chicago and Lynn Lewis in New York for giving me shelter and welcoming me into their home as family.

A very, very special thank you to James Tracy, Amy Sonnie and Bobby Lee who encouraged me to write this book and spent many hours guiding me through the process. Scott Crow for funding the first two edits of this book. Most of all I want to thank my nephew Tony Kerns for giving me shelter and financial help so I could write this book. And finally but not last my daughter Erica Thurman for her encouragement and love. And my mother Pauline Knight and my sister Geraldine Crowe who never gave up on me.

And to all oppressed people past, present and future who are fighting to make this world a better place to live.